Ethical Business Strategy

Ethical Business Strategy

R.K Biswas

ADHYAYAN

ADHYAYAN PUBLISHERS & DISTRIBUTORS

NEW DELHI (INDIA)

Published by
ADHYAYAN PUBLISHERS & DISTRIBUTORS
4378/4B, 105, J.M.D. House, Murari Lal Street
Ansari Road Darya Ganj, New Delhi - 110002
Ph.: 011-23263018, 011-23277156, Fax: 011-23280028
Email: adhyayanpublishers@yahoo.com

Ethical Business Strategy

Edition 2010
ISBN 978-81-8435-225-2

Printed in India

Published by Harish Chandra Yadav for Adhyayan Publishers & Distributors, Laser Typeseting at A.V. Rao and Printed at Tarun Offset Printers, Delhi

Preface

Business ethics is the behaviour that a business adheres to in its daily dealings with the world. The ethics of a particular business can be diverse. They apply not only to how the business interacts with the world at large, but also to their one-on-one dealings with a single customer. Many businesses have gained a bad reputation just by being in business. To some people, businesses are interested in making money, and that is the bottom line. It could be called capitalism in its purest form. Making money is not wrong in itself. It is the manner in which some businesses conduct themselves that brings up the question of ethical behaviour.

Many global businesses, including most of the major brands that the public use, can be seen not to think too highly of good business ethics. Many major brands have been fined millions for breaking ethical business laws. Business ethics should eliminate exploitation, from the sweat shop children who are making sneakers to the coffee serving staff who are being ripped off in wages. Business ethics can be applied to everything from the trees cut down to make the paper that a business sells to the ramifications of importing coffee from certain countries.

This is a lively and engaging textbook covering the foundations of business ethics and applying these theories, concepts and tools to each of the corporation's major stakeholders. It will help you identify and solve ethical dilemmas, understand why people behave the way they do, and help you design a culture that will promote ethical behaviour in your organisation. The emphasis is on common, real-life work situations, including hiring, managing, assessing performance, disciplining, firing, and providing incentives for staff, as well as producing quality products and services, and dealing effectively and fairly with customers, vendors, and other stakeholders.

Author

Contents

1

Introduction

Why should one be ethical? There is already something odd about this question. It is like asking, "Why are bachelors unmarried?" They are unmarried by definition. If they were married, they would not be bachelors. It is the same with ethics. To say that one *should* do something is another way of saying it is ethical. If it is not ethical, then one should not do it.

Perhaps when business people ask why they should be ethical, they have a different question in mind: what is the *motivation* for being good? Is their something in it for them?

It is perfectly all right to ask if there is a reward for being good, but this has nothing to do with *whether* one should be good. It makes no sense to try convince people that they should be good by pointing to the rewards that may follow.

Although ethics is not the same as self interest, business executives often want to be assured that it *is* the same. They want to make certain that "one can do well by doing good," meaning that one can succeed in business by being ethical.

There is no denying that one can often do well by doing good. An ethical company is more likely to build a good reputation, which is more likely to bring financial rewards over the long term. But good behaviour cannot be grounded in tangible reward alone.

There is a deeper confusion here, too. To look to ethics for motivation is to misunderstand what ethics is all about. It is like studying finance to find a reason to make money. So it is with ethics. Ethics teaches one how to be good, assuming one wants to be good.

It is important to know that one can normally do well by doing good. Otherwise ethical people could go into business only with a high risk of failure. Business ethics, however, addresses the opposite question: *how can one do good by doing well?* It begins with the premise that managers want to do something good with their lives and investigates how to accomplish this through business.

Granting that a business person's ultimate objective is to make the world better, how is this best achieved? A common view is that it is achieved by making as much money as possible. The best thing business people can do for society is to be good business people, which is to say, to maximise the company's profit.

Economist Milton Friedman articulates this view in an essay that is quite popular with business students, "The Social Responsibility of Business Is to Increase its Profits." Their sole task is to maximise profit for the company, subject to the limits of law and "rules of the game" that ensure "open and free competition without deception or fraud."

Friedman advances two main arguments for this position. First, corporate executives and directors are not *qualified* to do anything other than maximise profit. Business people are expert at making money, not at making social policy.

Second, and more fundamentally, corporate officers have no *right* to do anything other than maximise profit. If they invest company funds to train the chronically unemployed or reduce emissions below legal limits, they in effect levy a "tax" on the company's owners, employees and customers in order to accomplish a social purpose. But they have no right to spend other people's money on social welfare projects. At best, only elected representatives of the people have such authority. Sole proprietors can spend the company's money any way they want, since it is their money, but fiduciaries and hired managers have no such privilege. If they want to contribute to other social causes, they are free to join civic organisations and donate as much of their own money as they please.

It would be nice if the world were so simple. What happens, for example, when laws permit anti-social behaviour? Friedman's reply is that they must not, again on the libertarian principles just described. But suppose a hurricane hits a town and cuts off routes to the outside world. There is a desperate need for portable electric generators, and the only local seller takes the opportunity to charge an exorbitant price. Since this sort of price gouging is legal, the store manager has no right, on Friedman's view, to "tax" the owners by charging less than the market will bear.

This little example reveals two fallacies of Friedman's position. One is the idea that company officers somehow usurp authority when they act ethically at the expense of owners. Friedman admits that it is perfectly all right for a sole proprietor to sacrifice potential profit in order to be a decent human being. But suppose the owner has turned the business over to professional managers. Does ethical obligation to victims suddenly vanish? Is it permissible for the owner to exploit victims of disaster through agents, when it would be wrong to do it personally? Of course not. The owner cannot escape obligations simply by hiring someone to run the business.

This is not to say that managers should use company funds to support any cause that strikes the owners' fancy, such as the Irish Republican Army or the Sierra Club. The reason is that the owners have no obligation *as business people* to support these causes. They may have such an obligation as human beings, but it is not part of business ethics. Since owners hire managers specifically to run a business, they transfer only their business-related obligations, such as the obligation not to exploit disaster victims by price gouging. This is precisely why they should study business ethics as well as finance, marketing and operations!

The second major fallacy in Friedman's position is his misapplication of libertarian principles. He states that spending the owners' money in the service of ethics is coercion and therefore wrong, while operating in a free market to increase their wealth compromises no one's freedom and is therefore permissible. The electric generators provide a clear counter example.

The point is even sharper when a company decimates a community by moving a plant abroad. No one forced these people to work for the company in the first place. Yet the company limits their choices by putting them out of work, particularly the older ones, more than it limits stockholders' choices by reducing their dividends. To limit choices is to reduce freedom.

It is clear that maximising profit can "tax" the broader community no less than ethical choices can "tax" the owners. The business executive has a special obligation to owners, but it is not grounded in libertarian principles.

The inadequacy of Friedman's philosophy is particularly evident in international business, where there are fewer legal restrictions. A famous case study describes how the Nestlé Corporation marketed its infant formula in parts of Africa by hiring nurses in local clinics to recommend formula over breast feeding. The nurses convinced mothers that using formula was sophisticated and Western, while breast feeding was primitive and third-worldish. Unfortunately clean water was often unavailable to mix with the powdered formula, and babies often became ill. The company continued its marketing efforts despite worldwide protests and relented only after years of massive consumer boycotts of its products.

There is clearly an important element of truth in Friedman's position. Business people are not only at their best when making a profit, but in doing so they make an enormous positive contribution. Although Friedman says little about this in his essay, businesses provide a vast array of products and services that make life far better for millions worldwide. They can accomplish this largely through the expertise of managers who can run an efficient operation in a competitive environment. The primary ethical duty of managers is to apply their business skills and keep up the good work.

Rules of the Game

The task of business ethics, then, is to identify the duties that business people have as business people. What are these duties? One can begin with the most basic ones mentioned by Friedman: the duty to obey the law and the "rules of the game," which provide for "open and free competition without deception or fraud."

Yet even these basic obligations are disputed. Albert Carr's very popular essay, "Is Business Bluffing Ethical?" argues that deception, for example, is a legitimate part of business. Business, he says, is like a poker game.

Carr tells of a sales executive who made a political contribution he did not believe in, to keep an important client happy. When the executive told his wife about it, she was disappointed with her husband and insisted he should have stood up for his principles. The executive explained to her how he must humour clients to keep his job. She understood the dilemma but concluded that "something is wrong with business."

Carr not only expects the executive to make such choices but cautions him not to agonise over them. "If an executive allows himself to be torn between a decision based on business considerations and one based on his private ethical code, he exposes himself to a grave psychological strain."

Carr, like Friedman, has a point. Bluffing is expected in many business contexts, no less than in poker. What the poker analogy actually tells us, however, is that "deception" is not really deception when everyone expects it as part of the game. Nobody is deceived when advertisers say their product is the best on the market; everyone says that. So Carr does not actually defend deception. Hiding a card up one's sleeve, on the other hand, is truly deception because it breaks the rules of poker and no one is expecting it. Carr agrees that this sort of behaviour, which he calls "malicious deception," is wrong.

One problem with Carr's poker analogy is that he over extends it. In a poker game everyone knows the rules, but business situations can be very ambiguous. If a food processor places false labels on packaging, it is highly unclear that consumers are "in on the game" and expect this sort of thing. If Mom and Dad take the kids to school in the family car, it is hard to argue that they "expect" the car to be unsafe, as was the Ford Pinto with its famous exploding gas tank.

The example of the political contribution, as well as several others in his article, suggest that Carr is making an even stronger claim. He seems to argue that the business game justifies a whole range of activities beyond bluffing, such as perversion of the political process. The difficulty with this argument is that it proves too much. It implies that executives can do anything they want if it is part of a business game in which people play by the rules. This does not make it all right to participate in the racket, even if it is legal, which it is not. In fact, it is illegal precisely because it is the wrong kind of game to play.

The unavoidable fact is that some business games are good and some are bad. The right kind of competition, for example, can allow everyone to come out ahead, while the wrong kind can be destructive. When one plays the wrong game, then indeed "something is wrong with business." How does one know which game to play? There is a field that deals with this issue, and it is called ethics.

Carr compounds his error when he advises executives not to agonise over business decisions. He is right to say that they must not let personal sentiment cloud their judgment, particularly when it comes to such unpleasant duties as laying off employees or shutting down a plant. Hard decisions are part of life. Sometimes the game of business requires one to compromise oneself in order to make a larger contribution. Perhaps the sales executive can promote an exciting new product only by putting up with little indignities like kowtowing to his clients.

IMPRTANCE OF BUSINESS ETHICS

Even granting that business ethics is important, many seem to believe that there is no point in studying the subject. Ethics is something you feel, not something you think. Finance, marketing, operations, and even business law lend themselves to intellectual treatment, but ethics does not.

The idea that ethics has no intellectual content is odd indeed, considering that some of the most famous intellectuals in world history have given it a central place in their thought. Ethics is in fact a highly developed field that demands close reasoning. The Western tradition in particular has given rise to sophisticated deontological, teleological and consequentialist theories of right and wrong.

Even when they grant that ethics has intellectual content, people often say that studying the field will not change behaviour. Character is formed in early childhood, not during a professor's lecture.

If the suggestion here is that college-level study does not change behaviour, we should shut down the entire business school, not only the ethics course. Presumably the claim, then, is that studying finance and marketing can influence one's conduct, but studying ethics cannot. Where is the evidence for this view? The early origins of character do not prevent finance and marketing courses from influencing behaviour. Why cannot ethics courses also have an effect?

Ethics courses have a number of features that seem likely to influence behaviour. They provide a language and conceptual framework with which one can talk and think about ethical issues. Their emphasis on case studies helps to make one aware of the potential consequences of one's actions. They present ethical that theories help define what a valid ethical argument looks like. They teach one to make distinctions and avoid fallacies that are so common when people make decisions. They give one an opportunity to think through, at one's leisure, complex ethical issues that are likely to arise later, when there is no time to think.

None of this convinces one to be good, but it is useful to those who want to be good. It may also improve business conduct in general.

Ethics not only should be studied alongside management, but the two fields are closely related. Business management is all about making the right decisions. Ethics is all about making the right decisions. So what is the difference between the two? Management is concerned with how decisions affect the *company*, while ethics is concerned about how decisions affect *everything*. Management operates in the specialised context of the firm, while ethics operates in the general context of the world. A business manager cannot make the right decisions without understanding management in particular as well as ethics in general. Business ethics is management carried out in the real world. This is why business managers should study ethics.

Creation of Business Ethics

Before going forward in the design and implementation process, owners and managers need to decide what they are trying to accomplish through their business ethics program. An effective program will have specific, action–oriented, relevant, and timely performance measures. Also, essential to a business ethics program are mechanisms to measure the program's performance.

For the responsible business enterprise (RBE), an effective program is one that achieves expected outcomes and integrates well into the enterprise itself. As one ethics officer in a recent study observed, "Ethics programs become truly effective to the extent that they can evolve and plug into where a company is going." The study concludes that a well-integrated program is one that:

i) is aligned with an organisation's core beliefs;
ii) fits well with organisation systems, policies, and practices;
iii) addresses leadership priorities as well as employee expectations for ethics;
iv) is used by employees at all levels to guide decision–making and action; and
v) becomes a central part of an organisation's culture over time.

There are two principal areas to consider in setting business ethics program objectives:

i) How owners and managers think the organisational culture will be affected and
ii) What specific outcomes owners and managers desire from the program.

Essential Characteristics of Enterprises

A number of elements of organisational culture will give owners and managers a profile of the enterprise to help them design and implement an effective business ethics program. These include five characteristics of a highly effective organisation and eight influential cultural factors. When tracked and measured over time, these elements will be extremely valuable in evaluating program success.

i) Importance of Organisational Culture

The principal predictor of an effective business ethics program is the culture of the organisation itself. Responsible owners and managers will shape their management, ethics, compliance, and social responsibility practices to address nuances of the enterprise's organisational culture.

Organisational culture is shaped by the organisation's origin and history as well as the values, norms, and attitudes of its owners, managers, and other stakeholders.

Organisational culture influences what the organisation senses, cares about, and is capable of dealing with. It will influence how comfortable employees and agents are with engaging the stakeholders. Culture also is a source of conflict. As one noted scholar observed,

"The world is full of confrontations between people, groups, and nations who think, feel, and act differently. Responsible managers are challenged to find the common ground for enterprise stakeholders and to guide their employees and agents to meet their reasonable expectations.

ii) Characteristics of Organisational Culture

The first step in developing measures of an enterprise's organisational culture is to develop a profile of the enterprise as a whole. This profile can be captured in the following five characteristics:

i) Extent to which leaders and members alike embrace the organisation's core purpose and values, and are adept at preserving them while stimulating progress
ii) Extent to which leaders and members hold themselves responsible—and others accountable—for high standards
iii) Extent to which leaders encourage members to participate in organisational affairs
iv) Extent to which leaders and members have the knowledge they need when they need it
v) Extent to which conflict and mistakes made in good faith are seen as opportunities for learning and growth

iii) Indicators of Organisational Culture

More specific than the profile described above are a number of measurable indicators of organisational culture, which tend to be closely associated with expected business ethics program outcomes. Eight such influential factors are set forth below:

i) Perceiving that leadership cares about ethics and values as much as the bottom line
ii) Feeling safe to deliver bad news
iii) Feeling treated fairly
iv) Feeling valued as an employee
v) Not feeling pressured to compromise values
vi) Believing ethical behaviour is rewarded

vii) Believing unethical behaviour is punished

viii) Recognising whether the enterprise has an employee, community, or self-interest focus

Expected Program Outcomes

The primary purpose of a business ethics program is to help an enterprise address all four levels of its identity as an RBE. An effective business ethics program will include a performance measurement system that captures program outcomes that reflect the goals and objectives of the enterprise.

Tracking the following nine outcomes will help determine whether a business ethics program is effective for all four levels of identity:

i) How often violations of standards, including legal requirements, can be observed

ii) How often responsible business conduct issues are raised at the work place

iii) How often employees and agents speak in terms of core beliefs and standards

iv) How often employees and agents make decisions based on core beliefs and standards

v) How willing employees and agents are to seek advice on standards

vi) How willing employees and agents are to report observed or suspected violations

vii) How satisfied those who reported observed or suspected violations are with management's response

viii) How committed employees are to the enterprise

ix) How satisfied stakeholders are that the enterprise meets their expectations

Benchmarks and Baselines

When the data are collected and analysed, they may be used in a number of ways. They can give owners a picture of the culture, program processes, and business conduct of the enterprise. They can be used as baseline data for comparison with subsequent data. They can also be used to compare the findings with those of other similarly situated enterprises.

The first usage is helpful for owners and managers because it gives them a sense of how their employees and agents view the fundamental workings of the enterprise. Particularly valuable is comparing how managers, supervisors, and workers answer the same questions. Often, the answers are so different that one might wonder if the respondents work for different enterprises.

Where program evaluation is done on a regular basis—every one to three years, for example—the data serve as *baseline data*. Once a baseline of organisational culture, processes, and expected program outcomes is established, owners and managers can compare later data with the baseline to detect patterns and identify trends over time.

A final use is to compare the organisational culture, program processes, or expected program outcomes with other enterprises that establish benchmarks of practices or conduct. Benchmarking *can* be an effective practice if it compares program processes, such as code of conduct formats, business ethics office organisation, or help-line procedures.

Very little data are available publicly beyond large national surveys for program outcomes. Moreover, business ethics programs are so fundamental to the very identity of an enterprise that it would be difficult to make meaningful comparisons that take into account differing organisational culture, program process, and expected program outcomes.

Moreover, the real question is why owners and managers would want to spend valuable resources comparing their enterprise with other enterprises since the goal of a responsible business is to meet the reasonable expectations of their stakeholders, not to compare favourably with some other enterprise having different stakeholders. A favourable comparison alone does not help the enterprise learn what it is doing right, or even whether the data are accurately collected. In a culture of distrust, for example, employees will often refuse to answer a question about misconduct or will answer it incorrectly.

Understanding the Program Logic Model

Before beginning to design and implement a business ethics program, owners and managers must have a firm understanding of what will be required for the program to achieve its expected outcomes effectively, efficiently, and responsibly.

All management programs have common components. Typically, a situation presents a challenge to the enterprise. Owners and managers establish goals and objectives to meet the challenge. They develop a strategy and an action plan or program to achieve those goals. The action plan or program requires input in the form of resources, contributions, and investment. These activities and their output lead to expected program outcomes, the changes or results in people, enterprises, communities, or societies that occur over the short to long term.

A program logic model helps planners organise their thinking and encourage stakeholder engagement. It is a particularly effective means of graphically describing the elements of a business ethics program to the owners, senior management, employees and agents, and other stakeholders.Owners and managers can use the program logic model to stimulate dialogue and graphically portray how they envision their business ethics program working. A business ethics program logic model can be completed in four non–linear steps:

i) *Situation:* Describe the specific problem or issue. For example, a large customer may be requiring its downstream suppliers to comply with global standards.

ii) *Outcome:* Determine what the expected program outcomes are. That is, develop the measurable indicators that owners and managers want to accomplish over time that will address the problems or issues of their situation.

iii) *Process:* Develop the action plans that owners and managers will pursue to design and implement a business ethics program. They will want to address:

   a) *Input*: what they need to invest in terms of resources, including management attention

   b) *Activities:* what needs to be done to achieve the expected program outcomes, such as establishing standards, procedures, and expectations and conducting training and education

c) *Participants:* the stakeholders who will be involved in each activity

d) *Outputs*: what will actually be produced, such as, a code of conduct, three specific policies, or 50 percent of all employees trained within the first year

iv) Contributing factors, including assumptions: Describe the factors and assumptions that owners and managers considered in designing the business ethics program, such as the enterprise's capacity to draft a code of conduct or conduct training, the industry standards that apply, and the aspects of the organisational culture that they need to be concerned about.

SCANNING THE RELEVANT CONTEXT

Whether an economy is already developed or emerging, owners and managers in that economy should scan the relevant context of their enterprise to identify the pressures it places on the enterprise, its employees, and its agents. These pressures take five forms: threats, opportunities, demands, constraints, and uncertainties.

Importance of Context

All enterprises—whether large or small—strive to meet enterprise goals and objectives in a context of legal, economic, political, environmental, socio-cultural, and technological elements. Known as the *relevant context* of the enterprise, these elements bring pressures to bear on the enterprise, its employees, and its agents.

i) Legal Element

Government creates the legal framework in which market processes operate. As a sovereign entity, a state regulates private activities to protect or promote the general welfare of its citizens and residents.

Government regulation also defines how limited liability businesses, such as corporations, limited partnerships, and joint stock companies, are formed and what the limits of their liability are. Indeed, it may be that this tendency to define these roles and responsibilities in such detail is what discourages more discussion of corporate governance in terms of ethics and public policy. The very law that establishes minimum standards often comes to define the ceiling as well.

ii) Economic Element

An RBE must consider the nature of its market and the amount of trust that characterizes exchange transactions. In emerging market economies, the economic system is often unstable and characterised by frequent crises, causing businesses to seek short–term profits at the expense of long–term growth. Instability and lack of trust increase the cost of each transaction as the parties take expensive steps to protect themselves or avoid entering into a transaction at all. At the same time, the cost of regulation is often so high that shadow markets emerge, making it more difficult for the RBE to compete ethically.

Consumer expectations are a key economic factor. For example, consumers may be more or less discriminating. High quality may be more or less expected. Brand names may be more or less important. Employee economic expectations are also important. Privacy expectations for e-mail usage on company time also differ, as do employee expectations about policies such as the hiring of relatives.

iii) Political Element

In scanning its relevant context, an RBE needs to understand the kind and degree of government influence in the market, how laws and regulations come about, who has practical access to influencing them, and the degree of government control over the economy. Government presence in the trade and investment sector often restricts trade: decreasing competition, creating opportunities for corruption, and increasing costs to business.

iv) Environmental Element

The physical world in which we live forms the widest relevant context for the business enterprise to consider and its most controversial element. The planet itself is a system of interdependent ecosystems that has evolved over millennia in a process of creation and destruction.

Human beings are an integral part of this system and the first to influence consciously its evolution.

v) Socio–Cultural Element

In addition to organisational culture, each enterprise and its members operate within—and are products of—the broader cultures around them. Culture creates collective patterns of thinking, communicating, and acting that influence the decisions, processes, and activities of the enterprise itself. It influences the mental models that employees and agents bring to the job regarding fundamental issues of concern to managers, including the following five "dimensions of culture," developed by Geert Hofstede:

i) Social inequality, including the relationship with authority

ii) Relationship between the individual and the group

iii) Concepts of masculinity and femininity

iv) Ways of dealing with uncertainty, relating to the control of aggression and the expression of emotions

v) Long-term versus short–term orientation

Culture influences the decisions of owners and managers regarding a range of specific issues, including policies regarding conflict of interest, privacy, and nepotism.

vi) Technological Element

An important consideration in planning and implementing a business ethics program is the technology available to the enterprise and its stakeholders. Particularly important are computer and telecommunications capabilities. Telecommunications capability will influence how owners and managers exercise control and relay communications.

References

Albertson, Todd. (2007). *The Gods of Business: The Intersection of Faith and the Marketplace*. Los Angeles, CA: Trinity Alumni Press.

Behrman, Jack N. (1988). *Essays on Ethics in Business and the Professions*. Englewood Cliffs, NJ: Prentice Hall.

Bowie, Norman E. (1999). *Business Ethics, A Kantian Perspective*. Blackwell Publishing.

George, Richard T. de (1999). *Business Ethics*. Prentice Hall.

Hartman, Laura (2004). *Perspectives in Business Ethics*. Burr Ridge, IL: McGraw-Hill.

Harwood, Sterling (1996). *Business as Ethical and Business as Usual*. Belmont, CA: The Thomson Corporation.

2

Designing Business Ethics Infrastructure

When designing business ethics infrastructure, owners and managers will consider the nature of the enterprise—its size, its complexity, and the resources available to it. Over the past few decades, various offices and committees—for example, the business ethics officer and business ethics council—have developed to serve a number of necessary functions. These offices and committees meet the needs of Large, Complex Enterprises (LCEs), and it is valuable to describe them for those designing and implementing a business ethics program of any size.

Responsibility Functions

Leading enterprises, government agencies, and NGOs have found that an effective business ethics program addresses functions at seven levels of responsibility:

i) Overseeing the program at a high level

ii) Performing or coordinating the specific functions of the business ethics program

iii) Advising the responsible officer and business ethics officer and representing the enterprise as a whole

iv) Advising the responsible officer, business ethics officer, and employees and agents about specific professional ethics, compliance, and social responsibility issues, such as biomedical, engineering, or community issues

v) Linking various levels of the enterprise with a central ethics office

vi) Performing related executive and department functions

vii) Abiding by standards and procedures and striving to meet reasonable stakeholder expectations

Although these functions are discussed separately, the nature of the enterprise and its size, complexity, and resources may argue for combining any number of them. Informal channels and reporting relationships can also be integral parts of the design of a business ethics program.

The average SME may not have enough staff members to dedicate an employee or employees to each of the seven responsibility functions. For example, if an enterprise is large and complex, such as HCA Inc., an RBE may need a central coordinator and many high-level responsible individuals at dispersed facilities or regions. For an SME that has only one location, the function can be served by a high-level individual who has enough time to perform the duties—and is sufficiently detached from the issues raised—that he or she can be an effective channel for employees and agents seeking advice or reporting concerns.

Determining Systems of Authority and Accountability

Support for a business ethics program must start at the top of an enterprise. The following general elements of leadership are typically found in successful programs:

i) The owners or owner representatives ensure that the program provides them with adequate information regarding enterprise performance.

ii) The owners and managers set a tone of support for responsible business conduct.

iii) A high-level person is responsible for the business ethics program.

iv) The supervisors are responsible for how things are actually done in the enterprise.

Infrastructure for Owner Representatives

A business ethics program provides an information and reporting system for both the owners and the managers. An emerging corporate governance standard is that owner representatives are responsible for ensuring that they receive the information they need to prevent and detect wrongdoing.

While delegating authority to the chief executive officer (CEO) to conduct day–to–day operations, an RBE's board of directors must provide for systematic and rigorous monitoring of enterprise performance through an information and reporting system. Delegation of authority, however, does not relieve the board as a whole of its responsibility. It is important that the audit committee have unrestricted access to necessary records and personnel.

An audit committee is usually responsible for arranging for competent independent auditing. In this regard, it should be alert to any conflicts of interest that potential auditors might have, including conflicts stemming from their role as consultants.

Where managers sit on a board, an emerging best practice is for the audit committee to be composed wholly or predominantly of independent directors. If committee members are managers, or are closely allied with managers, the board may be unable to represent the owners without bias in favour of management.

High-Level Responsibility

A responsible officer may be an individual, a committee, or an individual supported by a committee. An RBE should avoid creating a situation in which no one is responsible because everyone is responsible. A single person needs to be tasked with ensuring that responsible business conduct becomes the norm at the enterprise.

For the business ethics program to be effective, the responsible officer, whether an individual or a group, should have a number of basic characteristics:

i) Be at a high level of responsibility in the organisation
ii) Have unrestricted access to the CEO and the board, or a designated board committee
iii) Have a high degree of trust and respect from senior management
iv) Have access to the resources necessary to ensure that the organisation has an effective program

v) Be given incentives and rewarded for proactively carrying out the roles and responsibilities of the office

vi) Have the skills to operate effectively with the media, public forums, government agencies, and the legal process

It is important that the person or group assigned responsibility for the business ethics program be at a high enough level to demonstrate the owners' and managers' commitment to the program. This requires that the person or group have substantial control over the enterprise or a substantial role in making policy.

The responsible officer has three major objectives:

i) Ensuring that the enterprise establishes adequate standards and procedures to guide employees and agents and to create reasonable stakeholder expectations

ii) Ensuring that these standards and expectations are institutionalised and enforced within the enterprise

iii) Evaluating and reporting on the enterprise's performance against these standards, procedures, and expectations

The reporting relationships of the responsible officer are critical. One key way in which owners and managers demonstrate support for a business ethics program is to demand regular reports on performance. Access of the responsible officer to the board and CEO serves a number of functions: it provides greater opportunity for responsible business conduct to be given due attention.

The responsible officer function may be served from any number of positions: an executive, a committee, an individual in charge of a business unit or major function, or someone with a substantial ownership interest. The position may be full-time or part–time, depending on the enterprise.

High-level responsibility may also be assigned for specific areas of ethics, compliance, and social responsibility. In an enterprise that does a lot of government contracting, a high-level person may be assigned to monitor that specific function.

In a highly regulated enterprise, legal demands may be such that a compliance officer should be appointed to deal only with compliance issues, in coordination with the ethics and social responsibility functions. In another enterprise, issues of responsibility to external stakeholders may be so demanding that a social responsibility officer should be appointed to deal with those issues, in close coordination with the responsible business conduct functions.

Business Ethics Officer

Independent of high-level responsibility for the business ethics program, a number of specific business ethics staff functions must be accomplished for the program to be effective. It is critical that a specific individual or individuals be assigned responsibility for these functions. Responsibilities for reporting to the owners are typically retained by the responsible officer. However, a best practice is for both the responsible officer and the business ethics officer to have access to the CEO and board.

i) Roles and Responsibility of the Business Ethics Officer

The business ethics officer is the staff officer responsible for the day-to-day operations of the business ethics program. Two practitioners have identified the following 12 functions of a business ethics officer:

1) Coordinate development and implementation of the business ethics program.
2) Establish and chair a business ethics council representing all levels of the enterprise.
3) Develop and maintain standards of conduct and procedures, as well as related policies, which will guide employees and agents and will foster reasonable stakeholder expectations.
4) Establish internal reporting channels, including, but not limited to, a help line that employees and agents may use to seek advice and report concerns without fear of retribution.
5) Establish or coordinate monitoring controls and measures to ensure that correct processes are established and followed.
6) Implement or coordinate enterprise-wide communication and training programs to ensure that all employees, agents, and other stakeholders are educated on the standards, procedures, and reasonable stakeholder expectations.
7) Coordinate or conduct inquiries and investigations to ensure proper follow-up on reports and resolution.

8) Delegate authority to conduct appropriate inquiries and investigations when necessary.
9) Monitor and evaluate the business ethics program for periodic modifications when needed.
10) Maintain a working knowledge of relevant issues, laws, regulations, and emerging standards of ethics, compliance, and responsibility through periodicals, seminars, training programs, and peer contact, including membership in professional associations.
11) Respond appropriately when a violation of these standards is uncovered, including making a direct report to the board or external agency if a violation of law or regulation is involved.
12) Report quarterly to the appropriate board committees on the status of the business ethics program, report to the CEO or appropriate board committees whenever necessary, and report to stakeholders annually.

ii) Location and Centralisation of Business Ethics Offices

The functions of the business ethics officer may be performed by one ethics officer out of a central location or may be decentralized. For example, the business ethics officer may be located at headquarters, or each plant may have a business ethics officer. The significant differences relate to responsibility and reporting.

The advantages of centralisation include a more consistent message, economies of scale in production and distribution, more effective monitoring of the program, and more uniform and efficient enforcement.

iii) Business Ethics Officer Qualifications

Business ethics officers generally have extensive experience throughout the enterprise over a number of years. They have developed personal networks that allow them to understand and relate well to the enterprise as issues arise. Owners and managers often bring in someone from the outside when there has been a pattern of serious misconduct or when they see the need for significant change in the organisational culture.

In terms of their operational experience, staff members from departments such as general business, finance, internal audit, and human resources tend to be tapped to be business ethics officers.

Business Ethics Council

The business ethics council serves principally as an adviser on setting policy, resolving issues, and monitoring the business ethics program. In larger enterprises, it often consists of representatives of executive management, including finance, general counsel, human resources, internal audit, quality, and public affairs. It is typically chaired by either the responsible officer or the business ethics officer. Wider participation may also contribute to greater employee acceptance of the program and its message.

A business ethics council should meet on a regular basis, perhaps monthly or quarterly. It raises issues of concern in the enterprise, reviews disposition of help–line requests for advice or reports of concerns, previews training materials, and recommends policy changes or program modifications. It meets on call when there are urgent matters to address, such as unforeseen conduct issues or a compliance violation that may require disclosure to government agencies.

If the business ethics officer is highly respected and has an extensive network of managers and specialists that he or she can turn to for advice, a business ethics council may not be especially valuable. The risk of not having such a council, however, is that the business ethics program lacks the formal acknowledgment that input from all levels of the enterprise is important to management.

Professional Ethics Council

The business ethics council is concerned with standards of conduct that affect the RBE as a whole. In many enterprises, well-developed bodies of professional ethics standards guide day-to-day operations.

In each of these areas, significant issues will arise that require the same sort of consultation and advice process that the business ethics council provides on more general issues. To address these more specific issues, an RBE might establish a professional ethics council.

If an enterprise wants to contribute to the welfare of its community as a whole, beyond its essential function as a business, it might appoint a community relations committee. Such a committee might identify specific community needs not met by government or civil society, coordinate with NGOs, and organise voluntary employee work projects. It would usually coordinate closely with the public affairs function to further enhance the reputation of the enterprise.

Business Conduct Representatives

An RBE must also determine how best to engage its employees and agents in its business ethics program. If the enterprise is large or complex, local personnel can be appointed to serve as advisers to local managers, employees, and agents and as channels for communication back to a central business ethics office.

Business conduct representatives generally report directly to both the senior manager at the location and the business ethics officer. They advise managers and other employees on standards, policies, procedures, and the business ethics program as a whole. They facilitate the functions of responsible business conduct at the local unit, such as training; monitoring, auditing, and investigating; providing employee incentives and discipline; and evaluating the program. Business conduct representatives must be familiar with enterprise standards, procedures, and expectations and all communications channels. They must be able to give unbiased advice that will not interfere with the conduct of their primary duties.

Related Executive and Department Functions

The business ethics officer is responsible for coordinating the enterprise's ethics, compliance, and social responsibility programs. This task requires that the business ethics program be integrated well with other enterprise functions. The chief financial officer, for example, is responsible for maintaining the enterprise's financial integrity, including all of its financial practices, books, and records.

An enterprise's internal auditor is closely involved in the enterprise's internal controls and processes. The internal auditor will be able to provide significant support to the business ethics officer by providing advice on internal controls and processes and by conducting inquiries and investigations. The business ethics officer will often turn to the chief legal officer for advice on legal requirements of a compliance program, due process requirements of inquiries and investigations, legal risk analysis, and possible program outcomes. In the minds of many employees, when one speaks of ethics one speaks of "fairness." Many ethics issues, therefore, involve human resources issues: assignments, compensation and benefits, discipline, employee assistance, and promotions. Other enterprise functions that the business ethics officer will work with closely are training, education, and development; environment, health, and safety; security; quality management; and operations and administration in general.

Individual Responsibility

To be a truly responsible business, the enterprise must articulate the responsibilities of all of its employees and agents in a positive, constructive manner. For owners, managers, and supervisors, this effort may involve complete awareness of the business ethics program itself. Owners, managers, and supervisors must demonstrate commitment to the program in all that they say and do. They are responsible for maintaining an organisational climate in which pressures to violate standards are minimised and incentives to achieve enterprise goals and objectives, pursue the enterprise purpose, and meet reasonable stakeholder expectations are high. For all employees and agents, their specific responsibilities under the business ethics program may require familiarising themselves with the standards, certifying receipt of the code and compliance with code requirements, attending scheduled training, participating in feedback sessions and investigations, and seeking advice and reporting concerns.

References

Seglin, Jeffrey L. (2003). *The Right Thing: Conscience, Profit and Personal Responsibility in Today's Business*. Spiro Press.

Solomon, Robert C. (1983). *Above the Bottom Line: An Introduction to Business Ethics*. Harcourt Trade Publishers.

Ulrich, Peter (2008). *Integrative Economic Ethics: Foundations of a Civilized Market Economy*. Cambridge: Cambridge University Press.

3

Ethical Behaviour in Organisations

"The question of ethics in business conduct has become one of the most challenging issues confronting corporate America in this era," is the conclusion of a recent Business Round table report. Indeed, support for this point abounds. Whether it be Wall Street, the defence industry, the savings and loan industry, or some local mom and pop operation, examples of unethical behaviour in business appear daily in the national and local media. In the last couple of years, virtually every major business and news periodical in the nation has depicted the business ethics of the 1980's as greedy, selfish distortions of the free enterprise system with excessive emphasis on personal wealth and fame. Ninety–four percent of the 1082 respondents to a 1988 Touche Ross survey of business executives, directors, and business school deans, said that the business community as a whole is troubled by ethical problems. Sixty–eight percent of the respondents said that they did not believe these ethical problems were overblown in the press.

Managing ethical behaviour is thus no doubt a critical social problem for business organisations. It is also a very complex problem which requires an in depth understanding of the many factors which contribute to employees' decisions to behave ethically or unethically.

Understanding Ethical Behaviour

Current behavioural research strongly supports a person-situation interaction explanation of human behaviour in which both individual and situational factors influence the behavioural choices made by individuals.

Individual Personality and Socialisation Factors

There is little doubt that personality and background will influence a person's ethical system—his or her system of ethical philosophies and behavioural patterns. Researchers have suggested three personality measures that may influence ethical behaviour. Ego strength is defined as an individual's ability to engage in self–directed activity and to manage tense situations. Machiavellianism is a measure of deceitfulness and duplicity.

Socialisation also seems to influence a person's ethical system. Researchers have identified sex role differences, religious beliefs, age, work experience and nationality as factors which may influence the ethical decisions made by individuals.

A critical socialisation factor for business managers is the influence of significant others. Research in social learning theory strongly supports the idea that we learn appropriate behaviour by modelling the behaviour of persons we perceive as important parents, siblings, peers, teachers, public officials, etc.

Ethical Philosophies and Decision Ideologies

A person's personality and socialisation will likely influence his or her ethical system. Both the content of an individual's ethical system — the norms that guide his or her ethical behaviour — and the individual's perceptions about when and how to apply these ethical norms will likely vary according to differences in personality and socialisation factors.

The content of one's ethical system, the network of ethical norms and principles one holds, constitutes a person's ethical philosophy. Social psychologists have contended for years that these normative structures influence the behavioural decisions made by individuals.

Cavanagh *et al.* identified three basic ethical philosophies, each of which represents a unique part of the total ethical situation faced by individuals in business organisations. The first is utilitarianism. The second philosophy is individual rights. This philosophy focuses on protecting individual rights such as the right to be informed, the right to free consent, the right to due process, etc. The third ethical philosophy is justice. Such an ethical system stresses social justice and the opportunity for all to pursue meaning and happiness in life. Researchers have accurately represent the ethical normative structures of individuals.

When and how persons apply their ethical philosophies will also vary from individual to individual. Forsyth contends that individuals differ in terms of the moral judgments they make, and that the actions they take resulting from these moral judgments also differ. He refers to these differences as ethical decision ideologies and says that they are based on two dimensions. First is idealism—the degree to which an individual believes that ethical behaviour always results in good outcomes. Second is relativism—the degree to which an individual believes that moral rules are situational. Persons high in both idealism and relativism are called situationists. They reject the use of universal or individual moral principles, preferring to analyse each situation and to determine appropriate moral behaviour based on this analysis. Subjectivists are individuals low in idealism and high in relativism. Absolutists are low in relativism but high in idealism. Finally, exceptionists, those low in both dimensions, believe in universal moral rules as guides, but are open to practical exceptions. Researchers have found that persons with different ethical decision ideologies vary in terms of how they integrate ethical information, how they judge their own ethical dilemmas, and how they judge the moral decisions of others.

Ethical Decision History

Social learning theorists contend that past decisions play a key role in current and future decisions. Once reinforced, a decision made by an individual will influence future decisions that he or she makes as ethical decisions are made and reinforced overtime, the individual develops an ethical decision history. Decision history is unique in the sense that it is both situational, because of its reinforcement foundation, and individual, because of the influence of the person's own ethical system and unique behavioural history.

Organisational Factors

Another set of factors influencing the ethical behaviour of employees exists in the organisational context. Researchers have concluded that a variety of organisational variables influence ethical behaviour among employees. Further, because of their immediate situational impact on employee behaviour, these variables, like with decision history, have been shown to have a strong direct influence on specific ethical decisions made by employees, usually overwhelming individual variables such as personality and socialisation.

The philosophies of top managers as well as immediate supervisors represent a critical organisational factor influencing the ethical behaviour of employees.

Another organisational factor is managerial behaviour. According to Nielsen, managers behaving unethically contrary to their ethical philosophies represents a serious limit to ethical reasoning in the firm. Much of the research cited in the above philosophies will have little impact on employees ethical behaviour unless they are supported by managerial behaviours which are consistent with these philosophies. If normative structures help explain behaviour patterns as social psychologists contend, then, conversely, norms not supported by appropriate behaviours are not likely to be accepted as legitimate by employees.

One of the most basic of management principles states that if you desire a certain behaviour, reinforce it. Another critical organisational variable that influences ethical behaviour is the firm's reinforcement system. Research in ethical behaviour strongly supports the conclusion that if ethical behaviour is desired, the performance measurement, appraisal and reward systems must be modified to account for ethical behaviour.

Several dimensions of the job itself may also influence the ethical behaviour of employees. Researchers believe that the more centrally located a job is in the communication network of the firm, the more ethical decisions will likely have to be made by the occupant of that job. Further, management often responds less severely to breaches of ethics by employees on whom they rely for technical expertise, because these employees represent a scarce resource for the firm.

External Forces

Two–thirds of the respondents to the Touche Ross survey also believed that competitive pressures represent a significant threat to American business ethics. Two key competitive factors which affect ethics were mentioned by these executives. One was the ever increasing competitive pressure to concentrate on short–term earnings. Another was related to the current multinational business environment with its varying ethical standards from country to country.

Volatile economic conditions, resource scarcity and pressures from stakeholders may also serve to undermine ethical behaviour in organisations. The ethical trap provided by external factors such as these is obvious. It places the firm in a position of having to choose between being an ethical role model for its industry and the environment in general or succumbing to the situational pressures and engaging in unethical practices.

This discrepancy in the opinions of the respondents to the Touche Ross survey as to whether high ethical standards enhance or detract from a firm's competitive position probably reflects the fact that ethical decisions have several potential competitive outcomes. Being ethical may directly increase a firm's profitability or it may directly decrease a firm's profitability. Further, ethical actions may have a less direct but nonetheless real effect on a firm's competitiveness. For example, decisions to recall a defective product or to withdraw from a market for moral reasons may have immediate costs but may also enhance a firm's image and thus its long-term profitability.

Behave Ethically

This is first and foremost in influencing ethical organisational behaviour. It is not the corporation itself that exerts moral responsibility, but rather the individual members of the corporation. Therefore, the institutionalisation of high ethical standards in corporations "stems from the character of persons who occupy the relevant positions." Managers cannot expect ethical behaviour from employees if they do not behave ethically themselves. Managers are the most significant role models in the organisational setting; thus they have a major socialising influence on lower level employees.

Behaving ethically may mean that a manager refuses to carry out unethical policies, threatens to blow the whistle, or actually blows the whistle. Individuals who take such actions often risk high anxiety and loss of potential livelihood. Thus, engaging in ethical behaviour may require a great deal of courage for the individual.

Screen Potential Employees

Since individuals are likely to face ethical issues most of their lives, there is little doubt that potential employees have significant ethical decision histories when they apply. Thus the first line of defense against unethical behaviour in the organisation is the employment process. There are several methods available to organisations for ethical screening. These techniques vary widely in terms of costs and benefits.

Background investigations, which can range in scope from simply checking resume information, calling references and requiring transcripts to hiring investigators, can be valuable tools in screening employees. Further, before conducting such an investigation, the organisation should inform the applicant and get his/her permission. On the other hand, since researchers have found that between 30% and 80% of all credentials may contain at least some misstatement of fact, it seems that firms would be well advised to require official transcripts, call references and former employers, etc. These methods are not very costly, and can help the company in avoiding problems down the road.

Other means for screening the ethics of employees were revealed in the Business KoundtaBle report. Johnson and Johnson includes its code to ethics in all of its recruiting material; and Norton specifies honesty and integrity as characteristics it wants search firms to screen for when finding applicants for positions with the firm.

There are both legal and ethical issues involved in screening employees. Its use in employment decisions has been seriously restricted by Federal legislation. Also, firms must be careful to consider the privacy rights of both potential and former employees when checking references, conducting background investigations, etc.

Develop a Meaningful Code of Ethics

Codes of ethics are probably the most visible sign of a company's ethical philosophy. In order for a code of ethics to be meaningful, it must clearly state its basic principles and expectations; it must realistically focus on the potential ethical dilemmas which may be faced by employees; it must be communicated to all employees; and it must be enforced. Further, a meaningful code of ethics cannot rely on blind obedience. It must be accepted and internalised by the employees who are required to implement it. To be most effective, a code should be developed and disseminated in an open, participative environment involving as many employees as possible.

All ten firms in the Business Roundtable report had strict codes of ethics. These firms stressed several factors related to successful institutionalisation of their codes including giving the codes to new employees as part of their selection and orientation, conducting seminars on the codes, and requiring communication of the codes at all levels. They stressed that communication of their codes takes place in open discussion environments where employees are encouraged to ask questions and make suggestions concerning the codes.

Provide Ethics Training

Employees need to have an experiential awareness of the types of ethical dilemmas they may face, and they need to know what actions to take in these dilemmas. Providing ethics training for employees is one key to increasing this awareness.

Ethics training normally begins with orientation sessions and open discussions of the firm's code of ethics. Employees should be encouraged to participate at a high level in these sessions as well as in other training that follows. Providing salespersons with scenarios involving improper gifts or kickback offers gives employees a chance to make ethical decisions in realistic situations and to discuss these decisions openly with peers, supervisors, etc. Organisations such as McDonnell Douglas and General Dynamics have used scenario training to transform their codes of ethics from simple documents to tools for training, education and communication about ethical standards.

Nielsen believes that this traditional approach' to ethics training may not be completely effective because it relies too heavily on ethical reasoning as an action (praxis) strategy for managing unethical behaviour. He says that traditional training approaches may improve an employee's intellectual understanding of what ethics is. However, there are many limitations which can impede the employee's ability to translate this intellectual understanding into practice. He suggests an alternative approach in which the actual ethical experiences, values and intuitions of the participants become the primary elements of ethics training.

Reinforce Ethical Behaviour

The reinforcement system of the company must support ethical behaviour. Employees should be rewarded for behaving ethically, and they should be punished for behaving unethically. This is not as simple as it sounds, however. It involves developing a clear understanding of how ethical behaviour is defined by the organisation, developing a system to measure and report ethical behaviour, and developing a performance appraisal and feedback system that includes ethical behaviour. General Mills uses integrity and social responsibility as a key factor in its performance appraisal and reward distribution decisions.

Effective reinforcement also involves being willing to make tough decisions in situations involving unethical behaviour. Remember, employees in positions to make ethical decisions are often those who play some central role in the organisation or on whom the organisation relies for technical expertise, etc. Disciplining employees who are critical to the organisation's success is not easy. And yet, successful management of ethical behaviour requires the resolve on management's part to be willing to severely punish unethical performance. There was consensus among the firms in the Business Round table on this point.

Mechanisms to Deal with Ethics

No cooperative effort for influencing ethical behaviour from within an organisation is going to be successful unless it is supported by the authority structure and culture of an organisation. One way to operationalise such support for ethical behaviour is by creating structural mechanisms for managing ethics. A variety of structural mechanisms designed to advise management about ethics, monitor ethical behaviour among employees, communicate ethical policies, serve as ombudsman for reporting ethical violations, etc., can be put into place in business organisations. Raelin calls for a professional ethical aide decamp for top managers.

In sum, ethical behaviour in business organisations is a complex, multifaceted problem with significant individual and situational dimensions. Effective management of ethical behaviour requires that organisations espouse ethics, expect ethical behaviour from managers, screen potential applicants effectively, provide meaningful ethical training for employees, create ethics units, measure ethics, report ethics, reward ethics and make the tough decisions when none of this works. Managers must often be willing to take risks in effectively implementing; such a system. Yes, managing ethical behaviour in business organisations is possible, but it is no easy task.

References

Badiou, A. (2001). *Ethics: An Essay on the Understanding of Evil*. London, Verso.

Berle, A. A. and G. C. Means (2003). *The Modern Corporation and Private Property*. New Jersey, Transaction Publishers.

Boatright, J. R. (1999). *Finance ethics. A companion to business ethics. R. E. Frederic*. Oxford, Blackwell: 153–163.

Brenkert, G. K. (1999). *Marketing ethics. A Companion to Business Ethics*. R. E. Frederic. Massachusetts, Blackwell: 178–193.

4

Responsible Business Enterprise

Across the globe, businesses are now expected to be responsible—to improve their business performance, make profits, and contribute to the economic progress of their communities by learning how to meet the reasonable expectations of their stakeholders: all those involved in, affected by, or able to influence the enterprise.

The responsible business enterprise (RBE) is an essential part of a market economy. Its responsibility is to serve the needs of customers while making a profit for its owners. It does so by cooperating well with its key stakeholders: employees, suppliers, and many others. Business ethics is an essential discipline of the RBE in a market economy. It guides the choices made and actions taken by the RBE in all its business conduct. The discipline of responsible business provides a toolkit of management practices to aid any enterprise in the responsible pursuit of its vision of a desired future.

The RBE is a collection of people who come together freely to pursue shared purposes. As a business, its purpose is to produce goods and services that customers freely choose to buy. As a responsible business, the enterprise - and its employees and other agents - takes responsibility for business choices made and actions taken as well as the results, impacts, and outcomes that follow. The RBE engages its stakeholders so that - through its business decisions and activities - it adds on balance value to its stakeholders.

Among the body of practices of the RBE, we distinguish between good management practices in general and specific ethics, compliance, and social responsibility management practices. This distinction is productive provided it is understood to be arbitrary. What we are really talking about are the practices management must be adept at, and pursue, if an enterprise is to be responsible. responsibility resources

Growth within an enterprise occurs most surely where its members respect and trust one another. The RBE pursues respect and trust through four integrated approaches: business and professional ethics, organizational ethics, corporate social responsibility, and corporate governance. These approaches underlie our inquiry into what it means for an enterprise to be responsible. They combine to form a fifth, integrating discipline: the discipline of the business ethics.

Each of these approaches represents a distinct body of theory and technique, which, when integrated, help us define the RBE. Taken together, these approaches describe a process that surfaces the essences of an enterprise where they are not yet clear and infuses them through all the enterprise says and does.

The RBE guides its employees and other agents through standards, procedures, and reasonable expectations based upon its core beliefs. It encourages and supports their responsible business conduct through structures, systems, and strategies designed and developed to foster reasonable stakeholder expectations and guide their employees and other agents. For the RBE, its strategies declare its purpose and core values. They establish how it will govern itself. They set boundaries to what its employees and other agents can do to achieve its purposes. They establish what its external stakeholders can expect from it by way of its business conduct.

In short, the discipline of responsible business establishes how an enterprise intends to succeed, what it assumes responsibility for, and how it holds itself accountable. Without the discipline such an approach instills, an enterprise risks a lack of focus. This discipline applies whether an enterprise is large and complex (LCE) or small to medium (SME).

Each of the following approaches to business ethics developed to meet specific ethics and policy issues.

— Corporate social responsibility grew because business ethics was not inclusive enough.

— Corporate governance grew because the shareholder-owners had limited legal liability, but no voice in management.
— Organizational ethics grew because organizations of all sorts had common issues of policy and structure.

We integrate all of these approaches as the 'discipline of the RBE' under the general term of business ethics.

Business ethics, then, is a tool to meet two important enterprise goals. It is a tool to help managers ensure that their employees and other agents comply with legal minimums. One must never lose sight of that goal. It is also a tool to help managers move beyond merely complying with rules and regulations. This allows them to set another, higher goal: to help lay the foundation for good business practices and functioning market economies for all.

In its classic sense, business and professional ethics is the pursuit of what is good in the production and exchange of goods and services. It defines business as a contributing member of society. Professional ethics more typically reflect trade association standards, peer pressure, and public opinion. Business ethics, in its narrowest sense, reflect a common sense of how the public is best served by a business.

Business and professional ethics are not recent events. Many professional codes have been around for a long time. An early example is the Hippocratic Oath, which provides, in part, "First, do no harm." But some codes or their provisions are new. Examples are biomedical ethics, especially the ethics of genetics, and cyber ethics, or the ethics of the Internet. Some codes are extensions, such as the ethics of health care, which reflects the political and economic trade-offs of providing social health care. Others are specific trade association ethics, such as journalism, advertising, or public relations. Still others reflect typical business functions such as human resources, finance, or procurement.

Organizational ethics serves as a bridge. It links the policy governance of the directors and the individual choices and actions of the enterprise's employees and other agents. Corporate social responsibility is the approach guiding the enterprise's aspirations for the future. Corporate governance is the approach of translating these aspirations into the policies of the owners. Organizational ethics is the means by which management guides its employees and other agents in their day-to-day business conduct.

Organizational ethics is the basis for a process that surfaces the essences of an enterprise and infuses those essences throughout all that it says and does. The process is typically called an 'ethics and compliance' initiative or program. It is an integral part being a 'RBE.' For an enterprise, an ethics and compliance initiative declares its social purpose and core values. It establishes what its stakeholders can expect of its business conduct. It influences how it will govern itself. It sets boundaries to what its employees and other agents can do to achieve shared purposes. If its context raises particular pressures, such as bribery or corruption, organizational ethics develops anti-corruption measures to combat them. In short, an ethics and compliance initiative establishes what an enterprise is responsible for and how it will hold itself accountable.

However, an ethics and compliance initiative also frees the moral imagination of employees and other agents. Goals and objectives are made clear. Boundaries are made known. Employees and other agents become free to pursue shared purposes by whatever means they have the capacity to dream. They must be able to justify their decisions and actions in terms of shared purposes, values and visions. But if individual choices and actions are otherwise within the boundaries set by the enterprise itself, they may proceed without fear, even if a mistake is made in good faith.

The classic 'narrow' formulation of business's social responsibility is the economist Milton Friedman's declaration that "the sole of purpose of business is making profits for its shareholders." While Friedman noted that this pursuit had to follow the law and social norms, he was explicitly opposed to holding business responsible for curing a variety of social ills not directly caused by it.

Those advocating increased social responsibility come from a variety of perspectives. Some resent corporate power and influence in general. Others want business to take "greater account of its social and environmental-as well as its financial-footprints." Others look at the power and affluence of corporations, especially in the industrialized West, and want to see them share that power and distribute that affluence in order to achieve their notion of 'social justice.'

There is no global shared definition of corporate social responsibility. A number of the main ones follow:

— *Business for Social Responsibility:* Business decision making linked to ethical values, compliance with legal requirements, and respect for people, communities, and the environment.

— *Canadian Business for Social Responsibility*: A company's commitment to operating in an economically and environmentally sustainable manner while recognizing the interests of its stakeholders.

— *CSR Europe*: A new business strategy in which companies conduct business responsibly by contributing to the economic health and sustainable development of the communities in which they operate, offer employees healthy, safe, and rewarding work conditions, offer quality, safe products, and services ... are accountable to stakeholders ... and provide a fair return to shareholders whilst fulfilling the above principles

Whatever their perspective, there is one principle on which most will agree. The responsible business cannot afford to ignore the legitimate interests of the stakeholders who make its success possible-owners, customers, employees, and suppliers. Another principle is perhaps more controversial for some than others. But most would also agree that the RBE cannot ignore those other stakeholders affected by its choice and actions-the community and environment. In a world of cable news and the Internet, a reputation can be made or undone through the simplest of choices and actions-and their impacts on others.

The RBE defines itself through the approach of corporate social responsibility (CSR). Through this process, the RBE defines itself in terms of core purpose, values, and vision of a valued future. It defines that vision by determining which stakeholders will be involved in, or affected by, its choices, actions, and their outcomes.

The RBE binds these elements of business life together as a sound set of beliefs about who it is and how the world works. It knows where it is and what challenges it chooses to address. It has a core to hold onto and a vision toward which to stimulate progress.

This is, then, is a mark of the RBE: that it knows who it is, what it aspires to, and who will be involved or affected along its way. The principal tool for the RBE is the process of 'stakeholder analysis.'

Corporate Governance

The dominant form of business in the global market economy is the business corporation. A fictional 'person,' the corporation is a government-chartered structure to organize collective effort. Its owners, the shareholders, have limited liability, by law, and may freely transfer their ownership shares. It is characterized by a separation of personal responsibility from business ownership. This has important ethical implications. While the owners are granted liability to the extent of their capital contributions, the enterprise itself is not relieved of the social roles and responsibilities that an unincorporated business must meet.

A board of directors represents the owners' interests, but a core of professionals manages the enterprise itself. The issues corporate governance addresses revolve around questions of who reflects the desires of shareholders, and how well they do so. The RBE defines how it will govern itself through the approach of corporate governance. Through this process, the RBE defines itself in terms of the three relationships: (1) owner-shareholders and their representatives, the board of directors; (2) the board of directors and management; and (3) controlling shareholders and minority shareholders.

A mark of the RBE is that it knows what ownership and management can expect from one another as stakeholders. In large part, external forces, such as laws, security regulations, and capital markets, define the viable options for corporate governance. This makes it all the more important for its governance to reflect, as much as possible, the aspirations of the enterprise itself and clearly defined responsibilities to the shareholders. But, to define the role of the board of directors broadly to meet social needs rather than represent the interests of its shareholders is to give "uncontrollable power" to the board. A poorly defined grant of discretion virtually invites abuse and further government intervention in the market.

Where ownership is separated from responsibility, shareholder liability is limited, as a matter of public policy, to encourage the free flow of capital. But what of the ethical responsibility of these owners? Does limited legal liability imply limited ethical responsibility? The global dialogue generally ignores this aspect of corporate ownership, though there is an increasingly significant movement for "socially responsible investing," which law does not wholly recognize as yet. Nonetheless, the RBE must take into account all the interests of it shareholders-ethical as well as legal-so we look here to the ethical responsibilities of stock ownership.

The RBE chooses and acts in ways that reflect the best interests of their owners. But these should be the interests of responsible citizens in their own right. This is one important political-economic-social implication for the RBE. Governance at substantial variance from the norms of society as a whole inevitably invites either shareholder disapproval or government intervention.

Corporate governance has been largely a matter of national or, in the case of the USA, state development until recently. On the international scene, there have been two major developments: the OECD published Guidelines for Corporate Governance and the influential body, the International Corporate Governance Network (ICGN), representing more than $6 trillion in assets, recommended that companies adopt the OECD guidelines "as amplified" by the ICGN.

In response to the growing importance of cross-border capital markets investments, the OECD adopted "Principles of Corporate Governance" (the "OECD Principles") in 1999. These principles are based upon the ethical premise that business leaders have an obligation to be fair, transparent, accountable and responsible in their conduct. The OECD Principles have been influential in shaping corporate governance codes in several countries throughout the world, including the Russian "Code of Corporate Governance," issued in April 2002.

The OECD Principles include recommendations on how an enterprise should operate its board of directors, set policies and procedures for internal supervision and control, and develop business long-term strategy. They set forth best practices of corporate governance including: instituting independent auditing; placing strong independent directors on boards of directors; following a clear and consistent concept of "conflict of interest"; guaranteeing shareholder rights, especially minority shareholders; establishing high standards of financial accountability and transparency; and commitment to honest and fair dealings with all elements of the business community.

Reflecting the interests of investors in responsible business, the ICGN made a number of far-reaching recommendations. In a "Working Kit" statement of corporate governance criteria, they addressed the issue of corporate citizenship in this manner:

1 *Corporate Objective*. The overriding objective of the corporation should be to optimize over time the returns to its shareholders. Where other considerations affect this objective, they should be clearly stated and disclosed. To achieve this objective, the corporation should endeavor to ensure the long-term viability of its business, and to manage effectively its relationships with stakeholders. (emphasis added)

9. *Corporate Citizenship*. Corporations should adhere to all applicable laws of the jurisdictions in which they operate. Boards that strive for active cooperation between corporations and stakeholders will be most likely to create wealth, employment and sustainable economies. They should disclose their policies on issues involving stakeholders, for example workplace and environmental matters.

The duties of individual members of the board of directors include actively monitoring the activities of the enterprise. In a 1996 case in the influential Delaware Chancery Court in the USA, the Chancellor held that:

> A director's obligation includes a duty to attempt in good faith to assure that a corporate information and reporting system... exists, and that failure to do so under some circumstances may, in theory at least, render a director liable for losses caused by noncompliance with applicable legal standards....

This case has been widely interpreted to require more effective organizational Corporate Responsibility Programs to prevent and detect criminal behavior. The decision, however, sets a relatively low standard to follow for individual directors to avoid personal liability.

Standards for Responsible Business

Global standards and expectations have developed over the last few decades. Governments, international institutions, transnational organizations, organized labor, and civil society conducted a global dialogue into what it means to be a responsible business enterprise.

This dialogue has not been complete. Many voices have not been heard or have been heard imperfectly. Moreover, there is an inherent tension between setting global standards and respecting local conditions. This being said, the standards and expectations of the last two decades reflect current best thinking and realistic best practices.

It is important to realize as well that these standards and expectations reflect the thinking and practices of market economies that are more or less successful at meeting the most urgent needs of their citizens. Many of them are honored in their breach to be sure. But as noted above, in developed market economies, breach is the exception not the rule. In fact, it is precisely because the behavior is not the norm is what makes the breach possible. Moreover, it does not follow that meeting these standards and expectations will necessarily lead to flourishing communities. Business can lead, but it cannot control the political-economic-social environments in which it operates.

On the other hand, it is highly doubtful that businesses and economies that do not aspire to-and largely meet-these standards and expectations will be invited to join a market economy in any enduring fashion. And if invited, it is highly unlikely that they will be able to participate fully in market economies that are largely characterized by these standards and these expectations.

Improving Business Performance

There is much support for the notion that the discipline of responsible business conduct outlined here contributes to improving business performance and expanding opportunities for growth. Principal benefits coming to an enterprise that implements a business ethics program are:

i) Enhanced reputation and goodwill

ii) Reduced risks

iii) Reduced costs

iv) Protection from unethical employees and agents

v) Enhanced performance, productivity, and competitive position
vi) Expanded access to capital, credit, and foreign investment
vii) Increased profits and sustained long-term growth
viii) Increased international respect

Enhanced Reputation and Goodwill

An enterprise's reputation for integrity is important for securing the loyalty of customers, for recruiting and retaining the most professional and honest employees, for becoming the business partner of choice, for winning local community acceptance, and for increasing access to capital and credit.

A business ethics program contributes to the enterprise's reputation for integrity. By giving adequate guidance to employees and agents, it ensures that they know what is responsible business conduct.

Reduced Risks

Every business, even if it strives to comply strictly with the law, is subject to risks such as these:

i) Being exposed to criminal prosecution for bribing a government contracting officer
ii) Being debarred from government contracting or a strategic partnership for an inappropriate gift or gratuity
iii) Having to recall products for failure to follow quality standards and procedures
iv) Having to clean up spills of toxic waste
v) Dealing with employee claims of sexual harassment
vi) Dealing with lost employee time for health and safety problems
vii) Being placed on a blacklist of international, national, or local organisations

An RBE develops processes with which it identifies, assesses, and manages the full range of factors that might pose a risk to social and financial performance. The processes include assessing risks, establishing adequate standards and procedures, training, and monitoring and auditing systems.

Reduced Costs

By providing employees clear guidelines on how to conduct day-to-day business in compliance with laws and ethics through a business ethics program, the RBE can reduce transaction costs. A business ethics program institutes procedures to detect and to prevent violations of the law and ethics.

The cost of bribery, kickbacks, and other forms of illegal or corrupt conduct is not only the amount paid. The full cost includes management effort to allocate time to work with officials, to maintain a second set of books, and to deal with the threat of extortion and blackmail.

Protection from Unethical Employees and Agents

It is not pleasant to contemplate, but the enterprise itself is often abused by its employees and agents. Embezzlement of enterprise funds is a major example. Cheating on time cards or carrying off supplies and tools, while relatively minor, add up to significant losses sustained every year by businesses—both large and small.

A business ethics program is designed to establish standards and procedures to prevent and detect violations of the trust put in employees. These specific processes may include establishing standards and procedures, monitoring and auditing systems, and reporting mechanisms.

However, at the heart of a business ethics program is the desire of owners and managers to foster the commitment of their employees to the welfare of the enterprise as a whole.

Enhanced Performance, Productivity, and Competitive Position

An RBE increases effectiveness and efficiency by enabling all stakeholders to work together closely on the basis of respect, shared values, and mutual trust. Such efforts lead to what one author calls "invisible savings" by reducing employee conduct that is harmful to the enterprise but difficult to detect.

Product quality may improve and transaction costs, such as contracting, may decline. For example, many large, complex enterprises (LCEs), most of which have business ethics programs, are developing preferred supplier lists to reduce the number of suppliers that they deal with. To ensure that there is no interruption in supplies and services, these LCEs require that their supply chains adopt the same good management practices that they follow, including a business ethics program.

Since, in the minds of most employees, ethics are essentially a matter of fairness, a business ethics program often increases employee morale. Better morale leads to increased productivity and innovation. It strengthens the enterprise's competitive position in its industry.

Expanded Access to Capital, Credit, and Foreign Investment

A business ethics program, including aggressive risk management processes, may increase an RBE's attractiveness to investors. Before making loans, international lending institutions and domestic banks perform due diligence on whether an enterprise is managed well. A business ethics program is designed to prevent and detect illegal and unethical practices. Financial institutions may view management as a worthy credit risk and allow access to capital at lower rates.

When entering new markets, foreign investors seek reliable partners who demonstrate integrity and operate on a transparent basis. A business ethics program reflecting global norms and values provides a common language between an enterprise and foreign investors.

Increased Profits and Sustained Long–term Growth

The discipline of responsible business conduct does not deliver instant results. However, a business ethics program—including infrastructure and processes for continuous monitoring of compliance with law and ethics.

Once an RBE has demonstrated its ability to detect and to prevent violations of the law and ethics, it tends to earn stakeholder confidence.

Increased International Respect

Adhering to the discipline of responsible business conduct can help enterprises gain access to international markets. It encourages compliance with laws and regulations that require a high level of transparency. When the generally accepted business practices of a community are based on sound standards and reasonable expectations, fair competition is the norm and the RBE can operate on a level playing field.

Recent research suggests that a business ethics program is particularly valuable in times of merger, acquisition, and restructuring. It is thought that the essential elements of a business ethics program may help members of often distinct organisational cultures manage their differences until they find common ground. These elements include core beliefs, standards, and procedures; high-level personnel responsible for the program; and dedicated resources to help employees seek advice.

Generating Social Capital

To define an RBE's social responsibility, we can think in terms of levels of social responsibility and try to appreciate the role of business in generating social capital. Thinking in terms of levels reminds us that if a business were to do no more than accomplish its essential business purpose of meeting the important needs of its customers, it would still be making a significant contribution to the common good.

Social Responsibility

The essential function of any business is to identify and meet the most important needs of its customers. In a free market, it is only by serving customers well that the enterprise will survive and prosper over time. An RBE is an essential part of a market economy, serving the needs of customers while making a profit for its owners and investors.

By entering the marketplace, an RBE does not cease to be a member of its community. Being in business is not a license to ignore community norms, values, and standards. An RBE uses good judgment in evaluating the social impact of its goods and services on customers and the community as a whole.

The socially responsible business works hard and competes fairly. It recognizes that to destroy the fabric of a marketplace to make a profit is short sighted. It does not abuse the public trust or degrade the environment, which we all rely on.

As a participant in markets and a member of its community the socially responsible business expresses its needs and concerns to government when appropriate. It avoids using its economic power to gain competitive advantage through political means.

Although the essential purpose of an RBE is to improve its business performance, to return a profit to its owners and investors, and to increase the prosperity of its community by meeting the reasonable expectations of its stakeholders, the RBE is nevertheless concerned about the quality of life in its communities.

Businesses often support literacy programs, local schools and colleges, and local infrastructure, such as water facilities, roads, or parks. Supporting literacy programs and education, for example, may lead to better employee applicants. Moreover, in some communities, a socially responsible business is expected or required to contribute a certain percentage of its income to institutions caring for the poor and needy.

In other communities, enterprises support such programs because such involvement makes stakeholders feel better about themselves and the enterprise. Through that contribution to the community, the enterprise not only enhanced its reputation, but also gave great pride to its employees.

Some people confuse this sense of social responsibility with what it means to be a socially responsible business. Nothing could be further from the truth. The important point to remember is that a business is socially responsible simply by virtue of effectively, efficiently, and responsibly meeting the reasonable expectations of its stakeholders.

Trust and Social Capital

Responsible business, as an essential part of a free market, is an investment in growth for a country as well as for an enterprise. Trust cannot be imposed; it must be earned.

Social capital is "performance based trust." It is "the ability of people to work together for common purposes in groups and organisations." Each participant in a market or society is responsible for contributing to the pattern of reasonable expectations. In such a community, trust will be rewarded. Social capital is the foundation of a successful market economy. The benefits of operating in a high-trust environment are many. Low–trust societies, by contrast, must fence in and isolate their workers with a series of bureaucratic rules."

Another scholar lists eight studies that demonstrate the link between values in general, trust in particular, and profitability. The link is based on an increase in creativity, support of management decisions, knowledge sharing, and pride, among other factors.

A climate of trust can be abused, however. Customers who are not attentive may purchase goods or services of poor quality. Employees may steal from their employers. Indeed, it is precisely because people put trust in others that many irresponsible business practices are possible. The discipline of responsible business conduct described in this and it leads owners and managers to build their enterprises with structures and systems that will compensate for a lack of trust. Over time, such conduct will lead to an organisational culture that is based on shared values and practices; more trust among stakeholders; and more effective, efficient, and profitable performance.

WORKING WITH LEADERS IN BUSINESS

Social capital also accrues through the efforts of civil society: organisations, such as trade groups, business associations, service clubs, charities, university faculty, and other non-governmental organisations (NGOs) that aim to hold business and government officials accountable. Business enterprises, in general, have the potential to be powerful and influential members of their communities. The RBE helps create the conditions for good public governance by promoting responsible business conduct—through self-regulation or through public dialogue with government officials.

FOUNDATION OF RESPONSIBLE BUSINESS CONDUCT

Responsible business conduct addresses the issues of ethics, compliance with laws and regulations, and social responsibility. Businesses face these issues every day in a market economy. Approaching responsible business conduct as a discipline broadens the thought processes of owners and managers by addressing the issues raised by business and professional ethics, organisational ethics, corporate social responsibility, and corporate governance.

A business ethics program provides a toolkit of leadership and management practices to aid any enterprise—large or small—in the responsible pursuit of its envisioned future. It helps owners and managers ensure that their employees and agents comply with applicable laws and regulations.

Special Opportunities for Small to Medium–sized Enterprises

Small to medium sized enterprises (SMEs) have an additional incentive to adopt the discipline of responsible business conduct: to create a wider commercial network. Where owners and managers embrace the global language of responsible business through a business ethics program, a network of business enterprises and supportive NGOs based on shared values is possible.

Emerging Global Standards

Particularly over the past two decades, a number of prominent business associations, NGOs, and international government institutions have developed a body of global standards for the responsible business. These emerging global standards are of four types:

i) A stakeholder engagement standard

ii) Substantive standards

iii) Management process standards

iv) Reporting standards

The major standards setting institutions are of three major types:

i) Business associations,

ii) Stakeholder groups, and

iii) International governmental organisations.

i) Business Associations

Business associations that set standards include the following:

i) *Caux Round Table:* A global network of business leaders committed to principled business leadership, the Caux Round Table believes that business has a crucial role in developing and promoting equitable solutions to key global issues.

ii) *International Chamber of Commerce:* The International Chamber of Commerce (ICC) champions the global economy as a force for economic growth, job creation, and prosperity. ICC activities cover a broad spectrum, from performing arbitration and dispute resolution to making the case for open trade, the market economy system, and business self-regulation. The ICC's report, *Extortion and Bribery in International Business Transactions*, is another resource that helps fight corruption and commercial crime.

iii) *Coalition for Environmentally Responsible Economies:* A U.S. coalition of environmental, investor, and advocacy groups working together for a sustainable future, the Coalition for Environmentally Responsible Economies (CERES) is committed to continuous environmental improvement.

iv) *Institute of Electrical and Electronics Engineers:* The Institute of Electrical and Electronics Engineers (IEEE) is a non-profit, technical professional association of more than 377,000 individual members in 150 countries.

Practices" organised under eight principles. The IEEE has an ethics committee and an ethics hot-line.

ii) Stakeholder Groups, Including Non-governmental Organisations

Stakeholder groups such as the following also set standards:

i) Interfaith Declaration: The Interfaith Declaration provides principles and guidelines to help practitioners identify the role they and their organisations should play in the community and to support problem solving.

ii) Global Reporting Initiative. The Global Reporting Initiative (GRI) was established in late 1997 with the mission of developing globally applicable guidelines for reporting on economic, environmental, and social performance, initially for corporations and eventually for any business, government entity, or NGO.

Convened by CERES in partnership with the United Nations Environment Programme, the GRI incorporates the active participation of corporations, NGOs, accounting organisations, business associations, and other stakeholders from around the world.

iii) *Social Accountability International:* A non-profit organisation, Social Accountability International (SAI) is dedicated to the development, implementation, and oversight of voluntary verifiable social accountability standards. SAI is committed to ensuring that standards and systems for verifying compliance with such standards are highly reputable and publicly accessible.

iv) *Global Sullivan Principles:* In 1977, the Rev. Leon H. Sullivan developed the "Sullivan Principles," a code of conduct for human rights and equal opportunity for companies operating in South Africa.

v) *International Corporate Governance Network:* A membership association, the International Corporate Governance Network is devoted to improving corporate governance internationally and providing a voice between investors and management.

vi) *Institute of Directors in Southern Africa:* In July 1993, the Institute of Directors in Southern Africa established the King Committee on Corporate Governance.

vii) *Institute of Social and Ethical Account Ability:* In 1999, the Institute of Social and Ethical Account Ability launched the AA1000 Framework. AA1000S is an accountability standard designed to help enterprises improve accountability and performance by learning through stakeholder engagement and by integrating their stakeholder engagement processes into daily activities.

iii) International Governmental Organisations

International governmental groups also set standards as shown below:

i) *International Labour Organisation:* The International Labour Organisation (ILO) is the U.N. agency that seeks to promote social justice and internationally recognised human and labour rights. The ILO formulates international labour standards in the form of conventions and recommendations setting minimum standards of basic labour rights: the freedom to associate, the right to organize, the right to collective bargaining, the abolition of forced labour, the right to equal opportunity and treatment, and other standards regulating conditions across the entire spectrum of work related issues.

ii) *Organisation for Economic Cooperation and Development:* Thirty countries sharing a commitment to democratic government and the market economy form the Organisation for Economic Cooperation and Development (OECD). Having active relationships with some 70 other countries, NGOs, and civil society, the OECD has a global reach. It plays a prominent role in fostering good governance in the public service and in corporate activity.

iii) U.N. Global Compact: U.N. Secretary-General Kofi Annan first proposed the Global Compact in an address to the World Economic Forum on January 31, 1999. Annan challenged business leaders to join an international initiative—the Global Compact—that would bring companies together with U.N. agencies, labour, and civil society to support nine principles in the areas of human rights, labour, and the environment.

iv) *U.S. Department of Commerce:* In cooperation with the Russian Chamber of Commerce and Industry, the U.S. Department of Commerce developed the *Basic Guidelines for Codes of Business Conduct* to reflect extensive input from Russian and U.S. trade organisations and businesses provided in the course of round tables and discussions conducted in Russia and the United States.

As the result of ongoing global dialogue between these institutions, a body of standards and expectations for responsible business has emerged. These standards address a number of areas of concern to responsible owners and managers:

i) Business conduct, including fair competition
ii) Community relations, including political involvement
iii) Corporate governance
iv) Environmental protection
v) Human rights

vi) Marketplace relations
vii) Workplace relations
viii) Accountability
ix) Reporting standards

Adopting Global Standards and Best Practices

When an enterprise designs a business ethics program, it is helpful to organise emerging standards and best practices as answers to eight questions owners and managers of any enterprise should ask themselves as they structure the enterprise.

The sample global standards and best practices are drawn from the experiences of LCEs. However, these resources are readily available to all enterprises, including SMEs, on the Internet, and they can aid in working out the answers for individual enterprises and serve to stimulate dialogue and inquiry.

In actual practice, even the LCEs borrow freely from the documents and experiences of other enterprises.

Challenges to the Responsible Business Enterprise

There are a number of issues of responsible business conduct to which the owners and managers of an RBE need to give special attention:

i) Relationships with government officials and entities
ii) Role of the private sector in the regulatory process
iii) Government contracting and procurement
iv) Role of voluntary action
v) Relationships with foreign governments and businesses

These five issues are central to what it means to be a responsible business enterprise.

Relationships with Government Officials and Entities

Governments establish the necessary conditions for economic stability, social progress, and environmental protection by adopting laws, policies, and practices that help markets perform independently, free of undue government interference. These conditions, sometimes referred to as "good public governance," help an economy grow according to market principles.

Good public governance respects human and property rights, supports the sanctity of contracts, protects residents, provides infrastructure that speeds the transportation of goods and services and supports the transmission of knowledge, and establishes a market–oriented legal framework and reliable judicial institutions that allow its residents to resolve conflicts.

Reducing Corruption, Bribery, and Extortion

To create the conditions necessary for good public governance, one must address the problem of corruption, from both the demand side and the supply side. Both government and the private sector are responsible for creating conditions for transparent business, and they should repudiate all corruption, bribery, and extortion. Leaders in business and government should work together to combat corruption.

One means of private–public sector cooperation is for business enterprises to recommend standards, procedures, and expectations to help the government administer laws and regulations in a transparent, accountable, and fair manner. This dialogue should aim to ensure that government administrative processes at all levels are fair, transparent, competitive, and informed.

Government administrative, licensing, inspection, and certification procedures intended to regulate business often create obstacles to business. Such administrative obstacles increase opportunities for public officials to demand bribes and favours.

Bribery, kickbacks, and other forms of illegal or corrupt conduct increase costs for an enterprise not only because of the payments involved but also because it requires management time and effort to work with officials, maintain secret accounting books, and address threats of extortion and blackmail.

Business associations in some emerging market economies have succeeded in influencing governments to adopt one–stop registration for new businesses. In the Russian Federation, for example, the Business Partnership of Seversk, a non-governmental organisation

(NGO), has worked with municipal authorities to increase transparency and to reduce administrative barriers. With input from the NGO, government authorities simplified procedures for leasing public property, which included streamlining procedures to resolve disputes and eliminating illegal fees.

To facilitate good public governance, the RBE can adopt standards, procedures, and expectations for conducting business with government officials and entities as part of its business ethics program. They should be based on knowledge of and respect for the specific rules that govern the conduct of public officials.

Encouraging Government Standards and Procedures

Responsible business leaders should encourage governments to adopt formal programs to guide the choices and actions of civil servants through established standards, procedures, and codes of conduct. These standards and procedures should address issues such as values of public service, conflicts of interest, use of public office for private gain, and acceptance of political contributions and bribes. Creating clear standards and procedures to which public officials are held accountable helps instill respect and public confidence in government institutions.

Government officials should be encouraged to go beyond simply setting standards and procedures. Civil servants should be hired and assigned transparently and should receive compensation adequate to support their families properly without resorting to corruption. Training and education should be provided to raise awareness of the devastating impact of corrupt practices on the functioning of public governance, as well as on economic growth and social capital. Finally, these standards and procedures must be enforced, and the government must respond appropriately when bribery and corruption are uncovered.

Business leaders must also recognize, however, that good public governance requires resources. Failure to pay business taxes when the government is trying to reform makes reform efforts virtually fruitless. Being part of the solution to this challenge of developing a market economy requires paying the enterprise's fair share of the cost of government.

Role of the Private Sector in the Regulatory Process

The ultimate objective of good public governance is to create conditions under which markets function independently and facilitate fair competition. These conditions help innovative, effective, and efficient enterprises succeed and grow while preventing inefficient enterprises from looting public resources.

Under conditions of good public governance, the private sector has a vital role in influencing the government to adopt laws, regulations, and practices designed to enable the market to function independently.

Improperly Influencing Government

There are several obstacles to good public governance, including practices that enable enterprises to influence government policy improperly. Enterprises operating in many markets have adopted the practice of forming patron relationships with individual public officials as a means of securing government contracts and preferential treatment.

Many large and successful enterprises strive to "capture" the state by securing the passage of laws or obtaining licenses that benefit them over other enterprises. What many think of as state capture is the effort of a firm to shape the laws, policies, and regulations of the state to its own advantage by providing illicit, illegitimate, and non–transparent private gains to public officials.

State capture is also a cause of poor public governance, because decrees issued to benefit one enterprise or organisation injure the economy as a whole by undermining competition. State capture seriously impedes the development of the rule of law. It creates conditions under which effective and efficient enterprises support ineffective and inefficient enterprises. World Bank studies show an association between state capture and poor governance in emerging market economies.

Properly Influencing Government

To foster stable conditions for economic growth, responsible business leaders should help establish clearly defined laws and practices regulating how businesses might influence government decision–making. RBEs conduct their business with government on a transparent basis.

Business associations provide a structure that enables private–sector leaders to find one voice and coordinate efforts. They provide the opportunity and leverage to influence lawmakers in an ethical and democratic manner. RBE leaders work with their business associations and trade groups to demand accountability of government and to create conditions for fair competition.

To maximise their leverage and influence, RBE leaders develop a national business agenda that promotes the goals and incorporates the interests of both large enterprises and small to medium-sized enterprises (SMEs)—and the public interest. RBEs publish their goals and strategies in the media in order to reach out to other businesses and solicit feedback from external stakeholders and civil society.

Private–sector lobbying efforts by RBEs promote and instill good public governance and respect for the rule of law. When a particular law or regulation is damaging to the market, RBEs seek to amend or replace it in a manner that respects the legislative process.

To strengthen this process, business associations often adopt a legislative advisory program, which analyses current legislation and assesses whether it meets the requirements and the needs of business.

RBE leaders work closely with civil society—including chambers of commerce, trade associations, industry associations, community advocacy groups, public interest groups, and other NGOs—to form alliances that help promote the national business agenda. Civil society "includes organisations, structures, and networks separate from the legislative, administrative, and judicial power of the state and, many would argue, from business but interacting with both in a variety of ways."

NGOs have a stake in the success of RBEs as entities that operate on a legal and transparent basis and fulfill their social responsibilities. NGOs also bring business and government leaders together to educate and train them in areas where they should work together on a more cooperative basis. On controversial issues, NGOs can serve as mediators between private and public–sector representatives.

Government Contracting and Procurement

When an RBE conducts business directly with a government official or entity, whether as a contractor, supplier, or in some other capacity, it should take steps to ensure that its relationships are transparent and ethical. It should abide by all laws; refrain from engaging in bribery, cronyism, or coercion; and avoid even the appearance of impropriety.

The success of public projects rests on sound government procurement practices that promote integrity, respect, fairness, and transparency. These practices also help create conditions for good public governance and the development of a market economy.

Challenges in Government Contracting

The process of government contracting and procurement poses a risk of corruption from both the demand side and the supply side. Corruption distorts the process by favouring one enterprise or group of enterprises over another. An obvious example is a contract for government procurement awarded to an enterprise in response to a bribe.

Under such conditions, a responsible enterprise cannot compete successfully for government contracts, even when it outperforms other companies in terms of quality and price. Nevertheless, when seeking a government contract, an RBE abides by all applicable laws, regulations, and stipulations of the tender.

Model Procurement Standards

The World Bank Group, which lends to governments to finance major restructuring of industries and development of infrastructure, has five basic guidelines that govern its procurement policies:

i) All goods and services needed to carry out the project must be procured with special consideration for economy and efficiency.

ii) The loan must be used to purchase only those goods and services needed to carry out the project.

iii) All qualified bidders from the bank's member countries have an equal opportunity to compete to participate in the bank's projects.

iv) The borrower must encourage the development of local contractors and manufacturers in borrowing countries.

v) The procurement process must be transparent.

The GPA is an accord entered into by 28 WTO member countries to provide market access to each other's government procurement of goods and services. It calls for governments to maintain transparency in government procurement by establishing standards in procurement procedures. These standards are designed to ensure consistency and predictability for enterprises. The notices are required to contain basic information necessary for enterprises to assess their interest in an opportunity and to prepare meaningful bids. The GPA sets out minimum time periods—usually 40 days—in which interested suppliers must submit bids.

The GPA addresses other procurement procedures, including qualification procedures, contract award decisions, and publication of procurement laws and regulations. The GPA also requires governments to maintain independent and impartial review bodies to hear supplier complaints.

Integrity Pacts

Another means of ensuring more transparency in government procurement and contracting is called an *integrity pact*, a concept developed by the NGO Transparency International in the mid 1990s. In the context of government procurement, an integrity pact is a formal pact or agreement between a government office inviting tenders and the enterprises intending to participate.

The key component of an integrity pact is transparency. All offers and payments made by an enterprise should be reported to members of the pact. The pact has preapproved sanctions for violations. Sanctions include denial or loss of the contract, forfeiture of bid security, liability for damages, or blacklisting by the government office.

Use of the integrity pact is slowly developing on a global basis, hindered by the expertise and funds needed to encourage governments and enterprises to enter into the agreement.

Role of Voluntary Action

The private sector has an economic interest in creating a trustworthy, stable, and reliable government capable of good public governance. Business enterprises, in general, have the potential to be powerful and influential members of their communities.

Beyond the contributions they make in producing goods and services to meet the needs of customers and consumers, businesses provide livelihoods for employees, other agents, and suppliers.

Leveling the Business Playing Field

Declarations of integrity are a form of voluntary action by enterprises designed to help promote a transparent business environment through responsible business conduct. They document a coalition of enterprises that are committed to fair business practices and showing leadership in this direction. Such declarations offer a means of bringing enterprises together with civil society and government officials and entities with the goal of developing a more transparent investment climate.

Industry–specific declarations of integrity may be an especially effective means of promoting responsible business conduct. In developing market economies, many industries, professions, and chambers of commerce accomplish much the same effect through codes of conduct that they voluntarily adopt and follow.

A prominent example in the United States is the Defense Industry Initiative, which was formed in 1986 to improve the responsible business conduct of defense contractors following a series of defense contracting scandals.

In emerging market economies, codes of conduct are being developed in many industry sectors, including engineering and banking.

Participating in Community Development

An RBE may also contribute to its community by participating in community economic development projects. Such projects promote cooperation between business and the local community. An enterprise that engages in a community economic development activity designs programs to train and employ local citizens.

Another avenue for an RBE is to work with a community foundation and local government to support community driven development. Development projects are designed to meet important community needs by engaging the community itself with help from donors to a local community foundation.

An RBE may encourage its employees to support philanthropic initiatives or to take part in volunteer programs. The RBE might also institute a release time policy, giving employees paid leave to take part in voluntary initiatives during business hours. Such an initiative will reinforce the enterprise's commitment to supporting employees and the community.

Forming Charitable Foundations

Leading multinational enterprises establish charitable foundations that donate funds to entities whose missions are consistent with the enterprise's values and vision. Such foundations provide funding for educational institutions and students through grants and scholarships, to improve the quality of education.

Relationships with Foreign Governments and Businesses

When engaging in international business, enterprises face government officials and entities, laws, customs, and cultural practices different from those in home markets. An enterprise will face new and different ethical dilemmas, which are shaped by local law, customs, and practices. An enterprise that seeks to conduct business in a foreign market or to form a joint venture with a foreign partner must first become knowledgeable of the local customs and practices.

While consciously striving to understand cultural and legal differences, an RBE remains focused on and committed to its core beliefs and standards, procedures, and expectations of responsible business conduct. It abides by the laws of its home country and all applicable foreign laws, whichever are stricter.

Combating Bribery of Foreign Officials

When doing business abroad, an enterprise should be aware of the strict rules and regulations that govern bribery in international transactions. In 1997, 34 nations signed the Convention on Combating Bribery of Foreign Public Officials in International Business Transactions. This convention, established by the Organisation for Economic Cooperation and Development (OECD), went into effect in 1999, and requires signatory nations to make the payment of bribes to foreign government officials a criminal offense.

Now enterprises operating in foreign markets are under increasing scrutiny and regulation in their home countries. For example, U.S. firms are governed by the Foreign Corrupt Practices Act (FCPA), which makes it unlawful to bribe foreign government officials to gain a business advantage. U.S. firms that conduct business internationally usually find it advisable to maintain rigorous corporate compliance programs to ensure that they comply with the FCPA and the laws of the other nations that are party to the OECD Convention.

The FCPA prohibits U.S. enterprises from using intermediaries such as an independent agent, joint venture, or foreign enterprise to make corrupt payments on the U.S. enterprise's behalf. They encourage these enterprises to practice due diligence when working with foreign enterprises.

Due diligence may come in the form of investigating foreign representatives and joint venture partners to determine their status as a local business. The FCPA encourages enterprises to be aware of red flags. Failure to comply with these provisions could lead to fines or imprisonment under U.S. law.

Adhering to Anti–Money Laundering Provisions

Using legitimate business to conceal the illegitimate origins of large sums of money—money laundering—has a destabilising effect on the enterprises involved, on domestic financial institutions, and on society as a whole. An economy that enables laundering of illegitimate funds is vulnerable to organised crime infiltrating financial institutions and legitimate businesses and aggravating corruption in government. However, having an image as a haven for money laundering will make it much harder to develop a reputation as a stable and secure environment for investment.

Enterprises working with a foreign partner, or even with a domestic partner that has connections with U.S. financial institutions, should be aware that the anti–money laundering regimes and reporting of suspicious activity that have been required for several years have been extended to additional categories of financial institutions.

While many countries, including emerging market economies, have similar anti–money laundering provisions, the U.S. provisions may affect foreign operations through requirements for due diligence for correspondent accounts and private banking accounts. Under these regulations, a broad range of financial institutions outside of the United States are subject to exercising due diligence under the U.S. anti–money laundering regime if they maintain a correspondent account in the United States.

Protecting the Environment

Finally, when engaging in business in a foreign market, an enterprise should be particularly sensitive to issues involving protection of the environment. An enterprise has a social responsibility to examine the impact its operations may have on the local environment and adopt global best practices for protecting the environment. Global best practices may be more demanding than local practices, but in a global environment, an RBE is expected to adopt the more stringent environmental protection requirements of the host government or its home government.

References

Collier, J. and R. Esteban (2007). "Corporate social responsibility and employee commitment". *Business Ethics: A European Review* 16(1). 19–33.

Cooter, R. and T. Ulen (1988). *Law and Economics*. New York, Harper Collins.

Cory, J. (2005). *Activist Business Ethics*. Boston, Springer.

5

Responsible Business Strategy

Enterprises of all sizes develop strategies to bring their resources together to achieve their goals and objectives. A business ethics program helps owners and managers improve their business performance, make profits, and contribute to the economic progress of their communities by meeting the reasonable expectations of their stakeholders.

To be effective over time, a business ethics program must be a formal plan, because it touches on all aspects of the enterprise—operations, human resources, communications, and marketing to name but a few. Formally planning a business ethics program ensures that owners and managers give due consideration to the enterprise's relevant context, organisational culture, and reasonable stakeholder expectations.

Busy managers need not fear that formal planning for a business ethics program will overwhelm daily operations because, as discussed below, they already have many elements in place. The planning process requires targeted stakeholder participation more than a large staff. A lack of program consistency will hurt employee morale and generate stakeholder cynicism.

Because of resource limitations, most small to medium-sized enterprises (SMEs) use informal program strategy and planning. SMEs are less apt to use formal teams and processes to set goals, objectives, strategies, and action plans than are large enterprises. Nonetheless, they can adapt the processes that follow to meet their circumstances.

These worksheets are intended to aid in designing and implementing a business ethics program. They are designed to be consistent with the principles of responsible management developed throughout these materials. For example, "Questions for the Responsible Business Enterprise", refers to emerging global standards and best practices.

Establishing the Nature of the Program

Owners and managers should define and communicate the purpose of the business ethics program as early as possible. Responsible management recognizes that an effective business ethics program touches every decision and activity of the enterprise. It guides patterns of thought, choice, and action that subtly shape the organisational culture of the enterprise.

Recent research suggests that "specific characteristics of the formal ethics and legal compliance program matter less than the broader perceptions of the program's orientation toward values and ethical aspirations." This research found that two factors are most important:

i) that ethics is perceived to be important to leadership—from executive through supervisor—and
ii) that employees believe they are treated fairly. It is particularly important that enterprise policies and management actions be consistent and that reward systems support ethical behaviour.

According to the research, familiarity with a code of conduct is relatively unimportant. Research and experience over the past 15 years suggest that a primary best practice is to design a business ethics program that goes beyond mere compliance.

Orientation of the Program

Program effectiveness is closely related to employees' perceptions of the orientation of a business ethics program. A business ethics program usually has one of four primary orientations. The orientation reflects owner and manager motivations in designing and implementing the program and is an important condition of program effectiveness.

The primary orientations are:

i) A *compliance-based:* approach, which "focuses primarily on preventing, detecting, and punishing violations of law"

ii) A *values-based:* approach, which "aims to define organisational values and encourage employee commitment to ethical aspirations"

iii) A *satisfying external stakeholders:* approach through which enterprises "hope to maintain or improve their public image and relationships with external stakeholders"

iv) A *protecting senior management:* approach, which "is introduced in part to protect owners and senior management from blame for ethical failures or legal problems"

These primary orientations are not mutually exclusive. As a single orientation, values based programs tend to be most effective. However, a business ethics program that includes aspects of compliance based programs and pays attention to satisfying external stakeholders is also valuable.

Considerations for the Small to Medium–sized Enterprise

Unlike large, complex enterprises (LCEs), the average SME is closely identified with its owners and managers. Thus SMEs must be particularly alert to designing a well balanced business ethics program. They have limited resources and staff, and, after all, it is *their* enterprise. Though in many cultures workers expect to be told what to do—even what to think—a program is more apt to succeed where workers are involved enough in its design to feel committed to it and where workers are willing to use individual judgment to apply its standards to the issues they face.

Owners and managers should, therefore, resist this temptation and engage their employees and other stakeholders as much as possible.

Building a Responsible Business Enterprise

Each enterprise has a unique ethical character. This character quietly guides what its members think, say, and do. It influences how external stakeholders view the enterprise. An enterprise's identity as an RBE has at least four levels compliance, risk management, reputation enhancement, and value added. Setting objectives in all four levels—and achieving them—is a goal of a business ethics program.

The identity of an RBE reflects how well it meets its responsibilities as a member of a community. Responsible business conduct—ethics, compliance, and social responsibility—is an essential part of this identity.

A business ethics program provides the essential core of the competitive strategy of an RBE. Programs more limited in purpose—called ethics and compliance programs—typically address the two lowest levels because compliance and risk management are the most obvious levels of identity.

However, a business ethics program addresses the higher levels as well—reputation enhancement and value added—in a systematic way.

A business ethics program helps an enterprise establish the essence of its identity in the community: its core purpose, core values, and envisioned future. It is an effective tool for establishing standards and procedures to ensure that enterprise values are reflected in all that employees and agents think, say, and do.

Compliance Level

Compliance means meeting all legal requirements through an effective program to prevent and detect misconduct. The average business enterprise faces myriad legal demands and constraints. Moreover, it is not enough that an enterprise intends to be law abiding. Good intentions alone will not safeguard an enterprise against the risks that its employees or agents will make mistakes or misbehave. Increasingly, compliance requires that an enterprise be able to demonstrate that it pursued management practices that are reasonably calculated to prevent and detect misconduct as a matter of policy. Demonstrating this may take the form of describing the formal structures and systems in place, having a compliance program with respect to competition law, or having an organisational culture that does not tolerate or encourage misconduct.

In the United States, the Federal Sentencing Guidelines for Organisations (FSGO) set forth seven minimum steps for an organisation to demonstrate that it has an effective program to prevent and detect criminal activity. These steps have come to constitute the minimum characteristics of an effective compliance program. In general, they require that an enterprise set forth adequate standards to guide its employees and agents. They must be communicated effectively to employees and agents. The enterprise must have means of knowing whether its employees and agents are following its standards.A high–level person must be responsible for executing the program. No high–level person can be involved in the misconduct.

In a similar vein, U.S. law requires many enterprises to have an anti–money laundering (AML) program, which has four elements:

i) Standards and Procedures,
ii) A compliance Officer,
iii) Training Procedures, and
iv) An external or internal audit.

Financial institutions are also required to have a specific customer identification program. Moreover, many U.S. government agencies, including the Department of Justice, the Department of Health and Human Services, and the Environmental Protection Agency, recommend, or in some circumstances require, compliance programs similar to the FSGO.

Australia has an alternative approach that looks to the culture of the enterprise. This approach is concerned with whether "a corporate culture existed within the body corporate that directed, encouraged, tolerated, or led to non–compliance with the relevant provision" or "failed to create and maintain a corporate culture that required compliance with the relevant provision."

It is generally recognized, however, that these standards and practices are not enough to create an effective business ethics program. With the exception of standards that are designed to prevent breaches of fiduciary duties, these standards and practices do not require that the enterprise meet the reasonable expectations of its stakeholders effectively or well.

Risk Management Level

To make ethics and compliance programs more effective, practitioners argue that enterprises should go beyond legal compliance and should systematically consider the industry and market risks that enterprises face. This involves assessing customer, supplier, and competition risk; examining enterprise policies, processes, and activities; and looking closely at organisational culture to establish whether there is a history of problems, disharmony, and conflict.

Reputation Enhancement Level

Damage to the enterprise's reputation has always been viewed as a reason to care about responsible business conduct. More recently, the kind and number of stakeholders that an enterprise needs to be concerned about has expanded to include media, non-governmental organisations (NGOs), and international institutions. Some enterprises strive to be RBEs simply to avoid criticism from this expanded stakeholder list.

It is more positive and creative to enhance one's reputation by making choices and acting in a manner such that one deserves a good reputation.

Value–Added Level

Increasingly, responsible business conduct includes adding value to the RBE's community through its decisions and activities. It is understood that the RBE strives to make a profit, but it is also expected to take into account its impact on its stakeholders. Though not often considered part of a business ethics program, producing goods and services of low quality may constitute consumer fraud or violate product liability laws. Producing low-quality goods does not enhance the enterprise's reputation—or contribute to employee pride or morale. And ultimately, producing low–quality goods or services adds little value to the community for the resources devoted to it.

An enterprise may add value to its community in many ways:

i) Serving the most important needs of its customers and consumers

ii) Providing gainful employment for its employees and agents, so that they can provide for their families and be responsible citizens
iii) Providing an adequate return to investors
iv) Purchasing goods and services from suppliers and service providers
v) Competing intensely, but fairly
vi) Forming strategic partnerships and alliances to create new business opportunities
vii) Supporting community infrastructure through taxes and fees
viii) Participating in the political process to improve market conditions
ix) Respecting the environment

To be truly responsible, an enterprise must fully embrace all four levels of identity.

Understanding an Enterprise's Strengths and Weaknesses

There is no one–size–fits–all business ethics program. The business ethics infrastructure should be designed to encourage responsible choices and actions, such that they become part of the culture of the enterprise itself over time. All enterprises have strengths and weaknesses. It is important to form enterprise strategies with a clear understanding of each.

The business ethics infrastructure and alignment practices selected by owners and managers must reflect enterprise strengths and must deal with enterprise weaknesses. Owners and managers should design a business ethics program that will accentuate enterprise strengths and will reform enterprise weaknesses.

Consider, for example, a recently privatised enterprise's reliance on personal relationships with government regulators to propel its success. In the short run, the enterprise may secure contracts or competitive advantages not warranted by the quality of its goods or services. As a result, research and development, quality programs, and effective marketing will tend to be undervalued and under used.

KNOWING THE STRUCTURAL COMPONENTS OF THE PROGRAM

When an enterprise undertakes to design a business ethics program, it seeks answers that go beyond what is required, at a minimum, to comply with law. It seeks broader, more creative answers based on emerging global standards and best practices.

Every enterprise already has some or all of the structural components of a business ethics program, even though no formal program may exist. What distinguishes the RBE is that its management works consciously to find those structures and systems that will ensure an *effective* program.

A well-designed and implemented business ethics program provides enterprise employees and agents with the guidance and information they need for effective, efficient, and responsible choices and actions. Research and experience over the past few decades suggest that an effective program contains the following nine structural components:

i) Standards and procedures to guide member behaviour and foster reasonable stakeholder expectations
ii) Adequate structures and systems that provide for authority, responsibility, accountability, and sustainability
iii) Communication of standards, procedures, and expectations to the enterprises members
iv) Programs that monitor and audit member conduct
v) Encouragement of members to seek advice and report concerns
vi) Due diligence in hiring, especially for sensitive positions in, for example, management, finance, and contracting
vii) Encouragement of members to follow standards and procedures
viii) Appropriate responses when standards and procedures are violated
ix) Regular evaluations of program effectiveness

PLANNING THE BUSINESS ETHICS PROGRAM

Five principles should drive the planning process and be honoured in implementation of the program itself.

Differentiate between Governance and Management

Owners and managers should sharply differentiate between the governance and management of an enterprise by delineating clear roles, responsibilities, and areas of accountability for policy-makers and managers. Even if the owner is the senior manager or if managers sit on a board of directors, the different roles and responsibilities need to be respected.

The source of a corporate board's authority is the owners of the enterprise. The board is the pivotal authority. Its authority is neither granted nor defined by management. Policies generated by the board control everything, both governance and management.

In practice, however, the board is often considered an adviser to management rather than its source of authority. In emerging market economies, lack of a strong voice for shareholders may lead to asset stripping and to rent diversion.

Build on Strengths

An RBE strives to be effective, efficient, and responsible through constructive and creative engagement with its stakeholders. To this end, it is helpful to identify and build on the core strengths of the organisation. The ultimate goal of a business ethics program is to appreciate an enterprise's strengths. This does not mean that weaknesses are ignored.

To the contrary, management applies what it knows about responsible business conduct to compensate for weaknesses. If employees are afraid to speak up, the enterprise provides effective mechanisms for employees to seek advice and report misconduct without fear of retaliation.

Entire Enterprise around Core Beliefs

Employees and agents can be empowered most effectively and safely when they share core beliefs. In fact, this may be the only way to empower employees and agents responsibly. If becoming an RBE is an enterprise's policy and goal, the effort must be based on core beliefs. Every employee and agent should be able to describe the core beliefs that will always guide his or her choices and actions, and should be able to define what constitutes success for the enterprise.

A few inspiring goals can provide further direction to employees and agents. They provide focus of effort and guide the allocation of resources. They order every task and form every structure so that the people involved know exactly how such tasks contribute to achieving the enterprise's goals and why such tasks are consistent with the core beliefs.

Delegate Authority across All Levels

To design and implement a business ethics program well, people at all levels of the enterprise must embrace it. A core of people, who are dispersed throughout the enterprise, must be personally responsible for seeing that the project succeeds.

Owners and managers must lead from the front, and it must be clear to all that responsible business conduct is their personal project. The various tasks of designing and implementing the business ethics program must be assigned throughout the enterprise. Moreover, these dispersed leaders must have the authority and resources they need to develop and exercise their responsibilities. Often, owners and managers will have to direct middle management and supervisors to gracefully release key employees from day–to–day operations to support the business ethics program.

Build in Continuous Improvement

A business ethics program involves so many levels of the enterprise and so many of its operations and functions that the process itself must be designed for continuous improvement. Moreover, other programs not usually considered part of a business ethics program should be integrated with it:

i) Quality management programs
ii) Preferred supplier programs that help an enterprise integrate responsible suppliers into its operational "family"
iii) Environmental, health, and safety programs to meet responsibilities to employees and the environment

iv) Human resource programs to be fair to employees

v) Sexual harassment programs to protect employees from abuse

vi) Labour–management programs to respect employee rights to collectively bargain

Engaging the Enterprise's Stakeholders

For an enterprise to be responsible, its management must understand what its stakeholders expect and work with them to form reasonable expectations. This is the case for every enterprise, whether it is an LCE or an SME. The discussion that follows addresses specific functions in the business ethics program design and implementation process with the owners and managers of an SME in mind.

An RBE recognizes that its stakeholders cannot be easily labelled. Some employees will also be customers or consumers of its goods or services. They may hold stock or options on stock in the enterprise and may be owners. They may live in communities affected by waste products leaked into the environment by the enterprise. They will have neighbours who have strong opinions about the way the enterprise does business. They look to government to provide good roads and other services, which may be compromised by business bribery and corruption.

To be effective, efficient, and responsible, an enterprise must have core beliefs that include an envisioned future of what its stakeholders can reasonably expect. The discipline of responsible business conduct helps owners and managers engage stakeholders to foster their reasonable expectations.

Engaging Stakeholders in the Design Process

Engaging stakeholders as early as possible applies the core beliefs and principles of an RBE, leads to better information on which to base design decisions, and builds goodwill with stakeholders. This principle applies to all enterprises—whether large or small.

Project objectives will be achieved only if the project is staffed with people who fully subscribe to them, have the knowledge they need when they need it, and are trusted throughout the enterprise. They generally maintain their normal duties within the enterprise during the design process.

Bringing together the Key Players

In the early stages of the project, there should be a designated *program catalyst*—usually an owner or the chief executive of the enterprise—who drives the project.

A *project officer* is primarily responsible for developing good ideas and approaches and inspiring people to embrace the eventual plan. He or she plays a prominent and important role in the early stages of the project. Ideally, the project officer is an employee familiar with the operations of the enterprise. The enterprise might then retain a trusted adviser, such as an accountant or attorney, or might employ an independent consultant.It is valuable for owners and managers to create special *working groups* to develop project objectives, scope of work, and roles and responsibilities. Such a group can serve as adviser, sounding board, and eyes and ears of the project as it progresses. With the assistance of staff, the working group can draft key documents and concept papers.

As the project progresses, the working group can serve as voice of the project. The group can communicate progress to the other stakeholders and test for reaction to date. Its members may be especially effective at evaluating the effectiveness of project communications.It is important to organise and build a *project network* to bring in more varied perspectives. Such a network is composed of various designated enterprise and external *stakeholder consultants*, who are individuals respected for their subject matter expertise or are recognised leaders and opinion molders. They become resources to whom the staff or working group can turn for information or reaction.

Using the RBE Worksheets

At the heart of the design and implementation of a business ethics program is a structured approach to:

i) Understand the pressures facing the enterprise, its employees, and its agents, and

ii) Understand its organisational culture, and

iii) Systematically enhance its strengths and reform its weaknesses through appropriate standards, structures, systems, and practices.

To use an RBE Worksheet, representative members of the enterprise and external stakeholders should form a working group. To include more voices, owners and managers might choose additional stakeholder representatives. Role-playing employees are often preferable to external stakeholders to preserve privacy and confidentiality.

Generally, an RBE Worksheet is a table with multiple elements or cells to stimulate dialogue and decision–making. The working group engages in a facilitated dialogue about each element of an RBE Worksheet, from the perspectives of the enterprise and its stakeholders. For each element in an RBE Worksheet, there will be at least one item of information of value to the enterprise.

For example, "Relevant Context Data Collection," RBE Worksheet 2, is composed of context element and stakeholder pressure cells. As the typical enterprise scans its relevant context, it will find *threats* from competition, potentially both foreign and domestic. Another threat might be a stagnant economy or an anticipated rise in interest rates or adverse currency fluctuation. There may also be *opportunities*, such as new products, markets, or strategic alliances. There will be economic *demands* to do certain things, such as meeting new quality standards. There will be some things the enterprise cannot do—that is, *constraints* established by law, reglulations, or industry norms and standards.

A working group should explore each cell, throwing out as many ideas as possible. All members should participate, and no idea should be considered unacceptable. Then they should go back over the ideas and discuss how the ideas may relate to one another.

If subject matter experts are engaged, they should contribute to, but not dictate, the conditions of dialogue. After analysing the data, the working group should take adequate time to reflect on what it means.

Adopting a Design, Review, and Approval Process

The RBE needs to take a number of practical steps before establishing a business ethics program. Owners and managers must determine the approach and orientation of its business ethics program. They must identify and engage all of an enterprise's stakeholders, foster their reasonable expectations, and order the enterprise's business affairs so that it improves its business performance and increases the prosperity of its community by meeting those expectations.

The responsible business enterprise operates at all four levels of identity: compliance, risk management, reputation enhancement, and value added. It meets all legal requirements through an effective program to prevent and detect misconduct.

A business ethics program has nine structural components that reflect global standards and best practices of responsible business conduct:

i) Standards and procedures to guide member behaviour and foster reasonable stakeholder expectations
ii) Adequate structures and systems that provide for authority, responsibility, accountability, and sustainability
iii) Communication of standards, procedures, and expectations to the enterprise's members
iv) Programs that monitor and audit member conduct
v) Encouragement of members to seek advice and report concerns
vi) Due diligence in hiring, especially for sensitive positions in, for example, management, finance, and contracting
vii) Encouragement of members to follow standards and procedures
viii) Appropriate responses when standards and procedures are violated
ix) Regular evaluations of program effectiveness

Many enterprises have published standards of responsible business behaviour. Over the past two decades, in particular, they have developed a body of best practices that enterprises in emerging market economies can consider and adapt for their circumstances.

References

Duska, R. (1999). *Employee Rights. A companion to business ethics*. R. E. Frederic. Oxford, Blackwell: 257–268.

Davidson, K. (2005). *Business Ethics. Ethics.* J. K. Roth. California, Salem Press Inc.: 181–187.

Dobson, J. (1997). *Finance Ethics: The Rationality of Virtue*. New York, Rowman & Littlefield Publishers, Inc.

Duska, R. (2007). *Contemporary Reflections on Business Ethics*. Boston, Springer.

Dutfield, G. and U. Sunthersanen (2008). *Global Intellectual Property Law*. Cheltenham, Edward Elgar.

6

Responsible Business in New Economy

Where a society wants to evolve from a command to a market economy, the challenges presented to individual enterprises can be daunting. All economies face the same fundamental issues of responsible business conduct—product quality, transparency in financial matters, workplace health and safety, protection of the environment, protection of workers, and compliance with laws and industry standards. However, they are magnified in both degree and kind when an entire society is making a rapid evolution toward a market economy.

Whereas the market economy has proved to be an essential condition for meeting the needs of the most people, valuable lessons have been learned along the way, often at great social cost. Societies and individual business enterprises have learned that it matters *how* profits are made, *how* wealth is distributed, and *whether* business can be sustained.

Business enterprises today are expected to meet standards of responsible business conduct that go beyond what had been expected traditionally. The pursuit of profits and economic progress is not a license to ignore community norms, values, and standards of respect, integrity, and quality.

Improved business performance, profits, and economic progress come to those who effectively and efficiently foster and meet the reasonable expectations of their primary stakeholders—customers, employees, suppliers, investors, and the environment, as well as the owners and managers themselves. Success for any business is ultimately measured in profits and losses, and the socially responsible business generates the capital and revenues required to operate and stay in business over the long haul. The socially irresponsible enterprise, however, fails to cover these costs because it is unable to meet the reasonable expectations of its stakeholders.

An RBE holds some enduring purpose beyond profit to define the enterprise and inspire and guide its employees and agents, because a purpose beyond profit sustains business enterprises. Enterprise purpose, moreover, helps employees and agents have a deeper understanding of the intent behind specific goals, measures, and actions.

RESPONSIBLE BUSINESS CONDUCT

An RBE is characterised by responsible business conduct at all four levels of its identity as an enterprise:

i) Compliance with the law
ii) Risk management
iii) Reputation enhancement
iv) Value added to the community

Responsible business conduct includes the choices and actions of owners, managers, employees, and agents that are:

i) Within their authority,
ii) Well informed,
iii) Intended to pursue the enterprise purpose and meet reasonable stakeholder expectations, and
iv) Sustainable over time.

Responsible business conduct allows an enterprise to improve its business performance, make profits, and contribute to the economic progress of its community.

Among the lessons learned by both business and government is that responsible business conduct can be encouraged by the structures and systems, procedures, and practices of responsible business conduct, often called *good corporate governance* or *best practices*.

A management tool owners and managers use to encourage responsible business conduct is commonly called a *business ethics program.* A business ethics program also helps owners and managers address the *triple bottom line:* the financial, social, and environmental results or impacts of the business's operations.

Business owners and managers have learned that a business ethics program helps owners and managers improve their business performance, make profits, and contribute to economic progress by better

i) Recognising political, economic, social, and technological pressures
ii) Understanding organisational culture: core beliefs, participation, responsibility, knowledge sharing, and methods of dealing with conflict
iii) Fostering reasonable stakeholder expectations
iv) Developing responsible management practices to meet stakeholder expectations
v) Learning from enterprise decisions and activities

Global Marketplace

The market economy has become increasingly global. Leaders in business, government, and non–governmental organisations (NGOs) now see global economic development as "the best way to increase prosperity within and among countries, and to create opportunities for millions of people, especially in the developing world, to secure a decent life for themselves and their children."

Businesses in emerging market economies face many challenges. For example, although no society *approves* of paying or accepting bribes, in societies where workers receive lower than subsistence level pay, "expediting fees" often become unapproved but *accepted* behaviour under local custom.

It describes processes reflecting emerging global standards, the design and implementation of a business ethics program requires extreme sensitivity to local norms, values, and standards. The program must recognise that management policies, standards, and procedures will be open to interpretation at all levels of the enterprise. However, a business ethics program takes a comprehensive approach. It recognizes such accepted behaviour as part of the challenges facing the enterprise and addresses such issues systemically.

A business ethics program does not set up either the enterprise or its employees and agents for failure. Rather, it strives to place the right people in the right positions in the enterprise to foster and meet reasonable stakeholder expectations as the surest means to improved business performance, profits, and economic progress. It starts from the assumption that enterprises are integral parts of their communities. It encourages them to work within the community to overcome the challenges of emerging market economies and contribute to community driven development.

Moreover, a business ethics program takes care not to mistake cultural, legal, or religious differences for a lack of ethics. In Islamic countries, for example, *mudaraba* may result in forms of payment that could be mistaken by those unfamiliar with the culture as inappropriate or unethical. A common cultural difference is the attitude toward hiring relatives. In some cultures, it is expected that owners and managers will hire relatives as a matter of course. In others, hiring relatives, which is known as *nepotism*, is discouraged or, in some circumstances, prohibited.

As long as businesses concentrate their attention and efforts on dealing with everyday challenges rather than striving to rise above them, they may be part of the problem. The ultimate issue for an RBE in an emerging market economy is whether it sees itself as part of the current problem or part of the solution.

Small to Medium–Sized Enterprise

The "place business should occupy in society" is a particularly challenging issue for the small to medium–sized enterprise (SME). Each SME is unique, often taking on the character of its owners and managers. There is surprisingly little research into the social responsibility of the SME.

SMEs in emerging markets are pioneers; they are plowing new ground as they contribute to developing a market economy. However, SMEs often lack the capital, staff, or time of large, complex enterprises (LCEs) to address many business issues. For example, tracking and complying with changing laws and regulations are relatively more costly for SMEs. SMEs seldom have the close relationships with government that LCEs have, especially those recently privatized. They are often unable to defend themselves against unreasonable decrees.

Though many of the best practices developed over the past two decades reflect the experiences of LCEs, there are a number of reasons why an SME might profit by adapting what the LCEs have learned:

i) The SME of today is more apt to become the LCE of tomorrow by adopting emerging global standards and adapting the best practices of successful LCEs.
ii) By adopting global standards and adapting best practices where they make sense, owners and managers are able to distinguish their SME from the competition.
iii) By understanding the basic principles and practices of the emerging global marketplace, owners and managers will be better able to recognise responsible business conduct issues earlier and to work with others to find solutions.
iv) Especially in a business environment that some perceive as high risk, first impressions count.
v) If an SME's people are conversant in the language of emerging global standards and best practices, they will be better able to speak the language of the global markets—and the opportunities to be found there.

Whereas the process of developing standards, procedures, and expectations is the same for all enterprises, the answers for each enterprise will depend on the size and complexity of the enterprise itself.

Moreover, SMEs will find that they need not act alone in adopting the world class standards, procedures, infrastructure, practices, and expectations described in these materials.

Transition to a Market Economy

For the enterprise in an emerging market economy struggling to make payroll, not to mention a profit, global economic development is, at once, an opportunity, a risk, and a challenge. As an opportunity, it offers tantalising prospects for new markets and access to international capital. The risk, however, is heightened competition and capital flow reversals from the slightest perceived political, economic, or social threat. The challenge is to learn from the experiences of successful businesses in market economies and to adapt them to overcome the legacies of the command economy. By learning from others' experiences, enterprises in emerging markets can contribute to the development of their own market economies and can join the global marketplace.

A business can influence—but not control—the political, economic, and social contexts in which it operates (its *relevant context*). Businesses and societies that do not meet or aspire to meet these global standards and expectations are unlikely to be ready to participate fully in the global marketplace.

Legacies of Central Planning

Central planning and state owned production characterised command economies. Resources were allocated by plan instead of by markets. Employment was generally full but effectively rationed through an internal passport system. Since planning was based on quantity, not quality, enterprises had little incentive for innovation; indeed, innovation or quality improvement was often punished with higher quotas or standards.

The law restricted or abolished human and property rights and the sanctity of contract. It limited individual rights rather than state power. The legal system lacked procedural and institutional tools to protect individual property and human rights and support the sanctity of contract. The legislative framework was not oriented toward private enterprise, and regulators, judges, and lawyers had little knowledge of, or experience in, free market concepts.

i) Economic Structure Precluded Competition, Entry, and Exit

The competition and innovation to meet the most important needs of customers and consumers, which characterise a market economy, were either unlawful or discouraged in command economies. For relative ease of control, state-owned enterprises tended to be large. New, competitive firms were few and were found more often in the unofficial or "shadow economy." Even state-owned enterprises survived through an informal bartering system, which remains, in large part, to this day. There was little competition from foreign producers, since trade relations were governed and restricted by planners.

In many emerging market economies, it is still relatively difficult for a firm to enter the market. The number of procedures, time of entry, and cost of entry vary, but they often greatly exceed what is required to set up an enterprise in a market economy. Enterprises are still expected to provide work and housing to some extent. When the high costs of entry are combined with low levels of "latent entrepreneurship", domestic competitive forces develop slowly, and open markets become less an opportunity than a threat.

ii) Producers Had Little Contact with Stakeholders

In a command economy, individual enterprises rarely had direct contact with suppliers, customers, or consumers—some of the stakeholders in a business enterprise. Entrepreneurs now have to develop these essential relationships, and many others, where none existed before:

i) *Customers and consumers:* Recently privatised enterprises had to shift their attention and efforts from satisfying the express preferences of planners—especially in heavy industry—to identifying and satisfying the preferences of customers and consumers.

ii) *Employees and agents:* In a centrally planned economy, where the quantity of goods produced is more important than their quality or fitness for customer purpose, managers could afford to look at employees as "hands." Independent judgment was often discouraged, and objectivity was seldom valued.

iii) *Suppliers and service providers:* With the abolition of central planning, an enterprise needs to develop a chain of suppliers, since it can now choose what suppliers and service providers it wants to work with—and vice versa.

iv) *Shareholders and owners:* Often, the privatisation methods used by many transitioning economies failed to ensure the presence of a *strategic owner*: a single shareholder with sufficient stake to provide motivation for monitoring management effectively.

v) *Lenders and investors:* Since in a command economy success for an enterprise was measured by meeting production quotas, businesses had little or no experience with the risk management aspects of lending and investing.

vi) *Government officials and agencies:* Under a command economy, the political system fundamentally favoured incumbent firms. At the local level, relationships were very close between politicians or bureaucrats and senior management. Though most state enterprises have by now been privatized, many of these close relationships between politicians and business managers remain in place

iii) Market–Oriented Legislative, Procedural, and Institutional Tools Did Not Exist

A market economy requires a high degree of confidence in the rule of law for business to meet its economic, social, and environmental responsibilities. In many emerging market economies, the vast majority of people do not trust one another. Transaction costs to protect one party from the other in such circumstances are much higher as a result.

A legal framework oriented toward free markets and reliable judicial institutions is essential for this confidence to develop over time. Such a framework will need

i) Contract laws
ii) Laws regarding the formation, operation, management, and dissolution of corporations
iii) Laws on privatisation
iv) Real estate laws
v) Laws against unfair competition
vi) Labour-management laws
vii) Tax laws
viii) Accounting and auditing standards
ix) Laws protecting intellectual property rights
x) Bankruptcy laws
xi) Environmental protection legislation and regulation

xii) Laws ensuring fiduciary responsibilities of managers and directors

xiii) Rules governing the rights and obligations of shareholders, managers, and boards of directors

xiv) Laws permitting class–action suits

A confusing, burdensome, or even unfair legislative and regulatory framework drives up the cost of setting up a business, dissuades investors, and provides a fertile ground for corruption. As one researcher observes, "Some critics even believe that regulations are intentionally drafted in a confusing manner to provide officials with more discretion." Such a framework is particularly damaging to the SME.

Even where laws and regulations are well drafted, they are often enforced unevenly—or ignored by the population—in practice.

It urges building an RBE from an ethical perspective, it is often the case that the state itself must actively support enterprises that are trying to be responsible but that find themselves at a competitive disadvantage. A key to introducing ethics in an emerging market economy, then, is to build a market–oriented legal framework and reliable judicial institutions. The RBE works with other leaders to influence government regulation to that end.

No less important than new laws, one researcher notes, is a judiciary proficient at interpreting and enforcing the law with integrity. The creation of effective dispute resolution mechanisms that can offer businesses transparent, predictable, and cost effective results is one of the most important steps a government can take to support market processes in an emerging market economy.

iv) Climate of Illegal Activity Persists

A final legacy of central planning is a climate of illegal activity. This legacy stems from the autocratic nature of the state and the unaccountability of its officials in a command economy, the remaining close ties between government and business, the incomplete legal and institutional reforms, the political and economic instability, and the ineffective implementation of market oriented reforms.

Among the consequences of a command economy was the emergence of an unofficial or "shadow economy," which was, by definition, unlawful. Current entry barriers increase the potential for administrative corruption, where entrepreneurs are tempted to pay bribes to overcome administrative barriers.

With the collapse of central planning and the lack of external constraints, insiders and managers during the transition to a market economy often took the opportunity to appropriate state owned enterprises for their benefit, leading to asset stripping and rent diversion.

Development of Market Oriented Institutions

To raise the living standards of its people, a society must provide the conditions for a functioning market. In a free market, the role of government in the market place is limited to protecting it from those who would attack or abuse it. "The state creates and preserves the environment in which the market can safely operate." A suitable institutional framework for a market economy would typically contain at least the following seven components:

i) A transparent regulatory system, including securities regulation
ii) A sophisticated accounting and banking profession
iii) A stock exchange with meaningful listing standards
iv) Labour–management regulations
v) A system of protection for intellectual property
vi) Effective legal and judiciary systems
vii) A broad–based tax system

Emerging market economies are struggling to provide these conditions to overcome the legacies of central planning, but institutional development takes time to design and implement. How successful an emerging economy is at developing an institutional framework depends, at least in part, on whether it had been a sovereign state, how well developed its institutions of public administration were, and how many valuable natural resources it can privatize.

Individual Business

The RBE recognizes its many roles and responsibilities in the community— and engages its stakeholders—adding as much value as possible. Through creativity, flexibility, and responsiveness in its day-to-day operations, it can add value to the community in many ways:

i) Serving the most important needs of its customers and consumers

ii) Providing gainful employment for its employees and agents, so that they can provide for their families and be responsible citizens

iii) Providing an adequate return to investors

iv) Purchasing goods and services from its suppliers and service providers

v) Competing intensely, but fairly

vi) Forming strategic partnerships and alliances to create new business opportunities

vii) Supporting community infrastructure through taxes and fees

viii) Participating in the political process to improve market conditions

ix) Respecting the environment

In an emerging market economy, an RBE must confront and rise above the legacies of a command economy. As a part of the solution to its economy's problems, it can participate in three essential ways: improving its business performance; helping build social capital in its economy; and working with leaders in business, government, and civil society to develop the essential market oriented legal framework and reliable judicial institutions.

Business Performance

An essential contribution of any business enterprise in the evolution to a market economy is to improve its own business performance. Performance can be improved by expanding and better engaging stakeholders as follows:

i) Establishing clear standards and procedures to guide employees and agents

ii) Focusing on anticipating and meeting the needs and desires of customers and consumers more effectively and efficiently

iii) Attracting, hiring, and bringing out the best in employees, suppliers, and service providers

iv) Establishing internal control mechanisms to build confidence among dispersed owners and investors

v) Developing and maintaining strategic alliances with enterprises sharing the same values

These best practices are at the heart of a business ethics program. They can significantly improve an enterprise's prospects for success. They can help an enterprise improve its reputation, manage its risk, protect itself from its own employees and agents, strengthen its competitive position, expand its access to capital and credit, increase profits, sustain long–term growth, and gain international respect.

Helping Build Social Capital

Respect, shared values, and mutual trust among individuals, businesses, NGOs, and government officials are the foundation of a market economy. To compete effectively and sustain economic growth, enterprises need social capital as well as financial capital. To contribute to this social capital, an RBE can

i) Make the case in its community for a market economy and the role of responsible business.

ii) Develop a reputation for meeting the reasonable expectations of its stakeholders.

iii) Agree to voluntary forms of alternative dispute resolution, such as mediation and arbitration, while domestic courts are formed.

iv) Take responsibility for its mistakes and misconduct.

v) Be willing to be held accountable for its mistakes and misconduct.

vi) Correct misunderstandings about its decisions and activities.

vii) Compete fairly with competition, both foreign and domestic.

How effectively, efficiently, and responsibly an enterprise is able to add value to its community depends, in large part, on how much its stakeholders trust one another.

An RBE helps government create the conditions for a market economy by promoting responsible business conduct—through self-regulation or by conducting a public dialogue with government officials and NGOs. Even where the legal framework of decrees, laws, and regulations is unfair, supporting the rule of law is an important practice for an RBE.

Responsible businesses can serve as a voice for the community. They can work with leaders in government, business, and NGOs to do the following:

i) Help develop the necessary institutional and legal frameworks for a market economy.
ii) Support initiatives to develop good public governance on the part of government itself.
iii) Strengthen NGOs to provide community-building services that business and government are unable to provide.

In economies where the government is unable to provide the social services a community requires, an RBE can work with other businesses and NGOs to identify community needs and can work with community–based organisations to provide such services. For example, the RBE can contribute supplies or services as a part of community–driven development, or it can contribute funds to community foundations. Some enterprises create their own charity programs or foundations or support volunteer work by employees.

Across the globe, businesses are expected to be responsible—to improve their performance, to make profits, and to contribute to the economic progress of their communities by learning how to meet the reasonable expectations of their stakeholders: their customers, employees, suppliers, investors, and the environment, among others.

An RBE in an emerging market economy has many legacies of a command economy to overcome while the state develops a legal framework and institutions that are market oriented. An RBE can participate in the transition to a market economy by improving its business performance; by helping build social capital in its economy; and by working with leaders in business, government, and civil society to develop the essential market oriented legal framework and reliable judicial institutions.

References

Armstrong, M. B. (2002). *Ethical Issues in Accounting. The Blackwell guide to business ethics*. N. E. Bowie. Oxford, Blackwell: 145–157.

Bradie, M. (1994). *The Secret Chain : Evolution and Ethics*. New York, State University of New York Press.

Friedman, K. S. (2003). *Myths of the Free market*. New York, Algora Publishing.

Galbraith, J. K. (1996). *The Good Society: The Humane Agenda*. Boston, Houghton-Mifflin Company.

Ulrich, P. (2008). *Integrative Economic Ethics: Foundations of a Civilized Market Economy*. Cambridge, Cambridge University Press.

7

Responsible Business: Standards and Procedures

The first question owners and managers of an RBE must ask themselves is, "What norms, values, and standards should we set to guide the members and foster reasonable expectations among thestakeholders?" Their answers define how the RBE will improve its performance, make profits, and increase the prosperity of its community by learning to meet the reasonable expectations of its stakeholders.

All enterprises set standards and procedures and foster stakeholder expectations. What distinguishes an RBE from other enterprises is that its owners and managers consciously develop the RBE's standards, procedures, and reasonable expectations as the surest route to improving performance, making profits, and contributing to economic progress.

A well–designed and well–implemented business ethics program provides all members of an enterprise with the guidance and information they need for effective, efficient, and responsible choices and actions. Employees and agents need to know what performance is expected of them. An effective business ethics program helps owners and managers develop standards, procedures, and expectations that establish the following:

i) Who has authority to do what within the enterprise

ii) Who is responsible for which decisions and activities

iii) How people will be held accountable for their individual choices and actions

iv) What stakeholders can reasonably expect from the enterprise

IMPORTANTANCE OF STANDARDS AND PROCEDURES

There are many reasons for an enterprise to set standards and procedures for its employees and agents and to foster reasonable expectations among its stakeholders. Standards, procedures, and expectations help focus the energy of employees and agents on achieving enterprise goals and objectives. The enterprise accumulates the social capital it needs to compete effectively, efficiently, and responsibly in global markets.

When standards, procedures, and expectations are not well established, owners and managers may not safely delegate their authority or expect stockholders to be well served. The enterprise will often find its members operating at cross-purposes, because it is not clear what is expected of them. Its strategies and action plans will lack focus and power. When standards, procedures, and expectations are unclear, it cannot readily measure its performance. Stakeholders, both internal and external, may become frustrated, cynical, or distant because their expectations have not been realized. Investor confidence, customer satisfaction, status as a preferred supplier or strategic partner, and employee morale will be at serious risk.

Standards, procedures, and expectations are more than just control mechanisms. They give the guidance employees and agents need so that they can choose and act confidently. A well-developed set actually provides a sense of stability. If owners and managers honour their own policies, employees and agents can act freely and confidently within defined boundaries.

Standards, procedures, and expectations establish criteria for the development of policies and performance measurement. They are the basis for determining whether choices or actions were made or taken in good faith or reflect good judgment.

RESPONSIBLE GOVERNANCE

There is a flow of authority, responsibility, and accountability throughout all enterprises. At the top of this flow are the owners or their representatives. The owners or representatives of an RBE follow a three-step process to establish policy guidelines for responsible governance. First, they delegate some measure of authority to managers. Next, they establish the purpose of the enterprise, including the value it brings to its community. Third, they establish clear limitations or constraints on the exercise of the authority they granted.

Following the responsible governance policies and procedures of the owners or their representatives, managers define methods, activities, conduct, and tasks for employees at all levels and for agents. They define the core beliefs of the enterprise and establish the guidance that employees and agents need to meet reasonable stakeholder expectations.

Responsible Governance Process

A social responsibility statement affirms the board's understanding that, while the board owes faithful attention to the interests of shareholders, it also must pay attention to social order and must see that the enterprise is a good member of a community. Finally, a director's conduct statement commits individual board members to ethical, businesslike, and lawful conduct.

Board–Management Delegation

In situations when owners are not actively engaged in an enterprise, they or their representatives will delegate a substantial amount of their authority to management. Responsible governance calls for such authority to be delegated to one person.

Under this arrangement, the lines of authority are clear. The owner representatives have one employee for operational purposes: the CEO. The CEO, in turn, is accountable to the board itself. The CEO will delegate some of his or her authority to other employees through standards, procedures, and expectations, but the CEO remains accountable to the board for all decisions made and actions taken.

Owner Expectations of Management Performance

Owner policies regarding management performance relate to the ends sought for the enterprise. The CEO is not entitled to make any choices or to take any actions that are not reasonably calculated to achieve the designated ends of the enterprise.

i) Policies Defining Ends

Responsible governance calls for precise definition of the ends of the enterprise. There are three components to an effective ends statement:

> "first, the *results* for which the [enterprise] exists; second, the *recipients* of those results; and third, the *relative worth* of those results."

At first glance, the *results* component relates to financial performance.

A range of performance results is possible: market share, long–term capital growth, profits, reliable income, and successful research and development. Owner representatives must take the desires of all owners into account to determine what the desired results of the enterprise are and how to communicate them to employees and other stakeholders.

The *recipients* component seems clear enough, since the owners are the recipients. However, as Carver notes, "owners do not all have the same interests, and the board represents all owners." The board must take into account the diverse interests of the owners. Although majority shareholders are entitled to a proportionate share of enterprise results, the board must not disproportionately benefit majority shareholders.

Finally, the *relative worth* component requires that the owner representatives prioritise among the results and recipients it has identified. Rarely will all owners have the same desired performance results. Others may be certain that their majority interest entitles them to disproportionate returns or influence over the board.

ii) Policies Defining Means

When the board is setting management limitations, Carver suggests they set "basic executive constraints".

Given that the ends of an RBE are ultimately to produce value for the owners, what about the many other considerations of the RBE, such as other stakeholders, the rule of law, and ethical conduct?

These are means issues. They are not the reason for the enterprise's existence, but they suggest how it may obtain its objectives. To preserve management flexibility, therefore, the board should establish policies that define the boundaries of management authority, rather than offer prescriptions for action.

Carver recommends that the board ask itself, "What management situations, activities, or decisions would be unacceptable to us even if they worked? Even if the ends are being achieved, what risks, ethical violations, and proprieties does the board want to put off limits?" When the board has answered these questions, responsible governance requires that it specify all the limitations it intends to place on management authority. The power of this approach is that management authority not expressly limited is, in effect, authorized.

Principles for Setting Management Standards, Procedures, and Expectations

Just as responsible governance at the board level involves setting ends and means for the executive, responsible management establishes a vision for the enterprise; goals and objectives; and standards, procedures, and expectations to guide enterprise employees and agents.

Strive toward Higher Standards

An enterprise should always strive toward higher standards. Expectations of an enterprise's ethical behaviour evolve constantly in response to changing market conditions, both regionally and globally. New values and beliefs emerge not only in the market, but also in the organisational culture and the personal lives of employees.

Consider Cultural Differences

Culture is difficult to measure, and dimensions of culture are even trickier to use in setting standards, procedures, and expectations. However, an increasing number of studies suggest that ethical decision-making processes differ, if not in the result, by country, nationality, and culture. Significant differences have been found in the matters of responsible business conduct, tone taken in addressing issues, and appropriate management responses to employee conduct.

Identify Exceptions from Home–Country Standards

Globalisation and the increase of cross-border trade and investment introduce enterprises to a wide range of cultures and values. The globalisation process includes increased pressure from civil society, the media, and governments from different nations. Enterprises are expected to abide by the ethical values of their home countries.

Sometimes, exceptions to standards, procedures, and expectations must be made when working with actors outside of the enterprise's home country.

Communicate Why

To ensure that the organisational culture is integrated and works toward an enterprise's goals and objectives, owners and managers should communicate not only the enterprise's standards, procedures, and expectations but also the reasons behind them.

Owners and managers should explain to employees and agents why complying with standards, procedures, and expectations is necessary and consistent with the enterprise's core beliefs. Managers should explain that such information could undermine a competitive advantage held by the enterprise and adversely affect its profitability. This explanation will impart perspective to the employee and help him or her understand the purpose behind the rules.

Include Employees in Setting Standards

Dialogue is required to set responsible standards, procedures, and expectations that fit the needs of the enterprise and its employees and agents. When developing or modifying a business ethics program, management must understand which responsible business conduct issues are of central importance to employees. Securing employee input is essential. Failure to do so can result in employee cynicism and erosion of trust between employees and management.

Clarify Operational and Ethical Responsibilities

The operational and ethical responsibilities of managers and other employees must be clearly expressed in codes of conduct and other aspects of a business ethics program. The relationship between employees and their supervisors should be governed by two central principles: authenticity and accountability. Authenticity requires honest communication about who is responsible for ethical practices, mistakes, and misconduct. An effective business ethics program sets forth these expectations and shows how the enterprise will address mistakes, misconduct, and misunderstandings.

Management Vision for the Enterprise

Responsible management defines the enterprise's core beliefs: its purpose beyond profit, its core values, and its envisioned future.

Two researchers, James Collins and Jerry Porras, found that what separates good companies from great ones, in large part, is the vision framework they provide their employees and aligning their choices and actions to that framework. The vision framework that they recommend has three components: a core purpose, core values, and an envisioned future.

Core Purpose

Without losing sight of returning value to the owners, responsible management establishes the fundamental reason for the existence of the enterprise in the form of a purpose statement that inspires its employees and agents. An enterprise purpose beyond profit helps define the enterprise. Unlike goals and objectives, the purpose is never actually achieved.

Purpose should be a succinct statement of how the enterprise intends to meet some important need of its community. A purpose statement captures the reasons that employees and agents are eager to go to work. It takes as given that owners want profits and that employees want livelihoods. But one can be certain that most employees do not go to work eager to make more money for the owners or even to earn their next pay check.

Defining an enterprise's purpose is not an easy process. Collins and Porras suggest describing what the enterprise does in business—its mission, for example—and then asking five times: "Why is that important?" Though deceptively simple, asking "Why is that important?" will help establish the value the enterprise brings to the community. This sense of value added becomes the ordering principle of all subsequent decisions and activities.

Core Values

Responsible management defines four or five values to guide the choices and actions for all employees and agents. These core values should be so fundamental to what the enterprise sees itself to be—and the way that it does business—that they will not be sacrificed for short–term gain.

Core values should reflect the fundamental qualities that the enterprise wants to use to guide employee and agent decisions and activities, but they should not be so far removed from the reality of the enterprise that they are impossible to follow or that they breed cynicism. Moreover, the process of defining core values will influence how they are understood, accepted, and followed.

Some enterprises arrive at their core values through a carefully crafted survey of their employees, including interviews and focus groups. Others establish advisory groups at various levels of the enterprise to work with a small working group to draft a set of values for further dialogue. A few enterprises survey all or most of their members plus many other stakeholders.

To bring to the surface enterprise values among employees, ask a simple question such as, "What would you tell a new employee who asks 'What does someone have to do to succeed around here?'"

Vision of a Desired Future

Responsible owners and managers visualise enterprise goals and objectives and the enterprise's role in the community over the long term. Goals should include responsibility to the community and to external stakeholders. They should incorporate relevant political, economic, and socio-cultural considerations. From this vision flow the goals, objectives, and expected outcomes of the enterprise's strategies and action plans.

Research suggests that there are two components to an effective envisioned future:

i) A specific goal that gives direction and meaning to enterprise decisions and activities and
ii) A vivid description of the desired future.

Management Standards, Procedures, and Expectations

Enterprises of all sorts and sizes are experiencing increasing pressure from home countries, international institutions, and non-governmental organisations to demonstrate responsible business conduct.

An RBE functions at four levels of identity: compliance, risk management, reputation enhancement, and value added to the community. Responsible management sets standards, procedures, and expectations at all four levels to give adequate guidance to employees and agents. These standards, procedures, and expectations tend to foster reasonable external stakeholder expectations of enterprise performance.

Guiding Principles

Enterprises will find value in establishing a number of general principles to guide employees and agents. With the core beliefs providing the basis, a statement of general principles aids employees and agents in making choices and taking action.

For some enterprises, like Royal Dutch/Shell, its fundamental guiding document is its "Statement of General Business Principles." Another executive–level set of guiding principles to consider is the U.N. Global Compact.

Statements of guiding principles tend to be accessible to employees and agents because they are considerably shorter than the average code of conduct. These principles may be one sentence statements or short paragraphs, but usually no longer.

Using Royal Dutch/Shell as an example, an enterprise might set forth its basic principles under nine topics:

i) Objectives;
ii) Responsibilities to stakeholders;
iii) Economic principles;
iv) Business integrity;
v) Political activities;
vi) Health, safety, and the Environment;
vii) Community,
viii) Competition; and
ix) Full relevant disclosure.

Shell begins with a general preamble that states the purpose of the principles themselves.

The first principle sets forth a general statement of the *objectives* of the enterprise. These closely track its core purpose. The second principle sets forth the *responsibilities* that it believes it owes its primary stakeholders: shareholders, customers, employees, those with whom it does business, and society as a whole, which includes the environment. These descriptions are, for the most part, one or two sentences each.

The third principle sets *economic* principles to guide its employees and agents. Shell notes that profitability and a strong financial foundation are fundamental to meeting its responsibilities.

Shell's fourth principle addresses its notion of *business integrity*. Shell maintains that its companies "insist on honesty, integrity, and fairness in all aspects of their business and expect the same in their relationships with all those with whom they do business." Going into somewhat more detail than a statement of principle, Shell's business integrity principle expressly addresses bribery, conflicts of interest, and maintaining accurate books and records.

Shell's fifth principle, regarding *political activities*, reinforces its sense of social responsibility and restricts its companies and individual employees in their political activities.

Shell's sixth principle addresses its commitment to contribute to *sustainable development* and its "systematic approach to healt' safety, and environmental management in order to achieve continuous performance improvement."

Shell's seventh principle addresses its relationship with the *community*. It expressly notes that its most important contribution is to pursue what we term its core purpose and its envisioned future as a business as effectively as possible.

Shell's eighth principle is express support for the *competition* inherent in free enterprise.

Finally, Shell commits to providing *full relevant information* about its "activities to legitimately interested parties, subject to any overriding considerations of business confidentiality and cost."

Non-governmental organisations (NGOs), while applauding Shell's statement in general, have noted, for example, that it does not specifically address a number of international conventions, notably the Universal Declaration of Human Rights, as well as the Tripartite Declaration of Principles of the International Labour Organisation.

Another common approach to a guiding set of principles is to list the enterprise's core values with a number of guiding principles or practices below each value. An example is United Technologies Corporation, which sets forth five "Commitments": "performance, pioneering innovation, personal development, social responsibility, and share owner value". The value of this approach is that it demonstrates the significance of a few core values, while using principles and practices to define them and to provide concrete examples in one document.

Management may also consider any number of other general principles for ideas. One set to consider is the "Principles for Business" of the Caux Round Table, which are widely considered a good starting point for developing an enterprise's sense of ethical and responsible business conduct.

Code of Conduct

A code of conduct is often the primary means by which management gives guidance to its employees and agents as to what is expected of them by way of business conduct. Indeed, among large enterprises globally, most now have some form of code of conduct.

A code demonstrates management's commitment to meeting all applicable industry practices and government regulations. Its target audience is the enterprise as a whole.

A code of conduct addresses minimum standards of conduct and procedures to reduce the enterprise's risk of liability and damage to its reputation. A code of conduct also goes beyond these minimums to guide employees and agents toward enhancing the enterprise's reputation and adding genuine value to its community.

It is important not to place too much significance on a code of conduct standing alone. Most research suggests that a code is important less for its specific provisions than as part of a program or strategy to encourage responsible business conduct.

As part of a business ethics program, however, a code is a central component of a process by which the enterprise engages its stakeholders, both internal and external. Increasingly, codes are an essential part of an ongoing dialogue designed to shape programs.

An enterprise should carefully examine its relevant context when deciding on the scope of its code of conduct. It should consider the priorities of its community and external stakeholders; the state of decrees, laws, and regulations; and industry standards. It should also show respect for national and organisational culture.

i) Compliance with the Law

When designing a business ethics program, an enterprise must ensure that it complies with all laws and regulations that govern its area of commerce: local, foreign, and international. The codes themselves tend not to set forth the details of the law. However, they will set the general policy of complying with all laws, and they may refer to laws that have specific application to the enterprise's business conduct such as corporate governance, workplace practices, and relationships with government officials.

The general nature of a code of conduct—as well as the issues addressed—differ widely between the European Union and the United States. Codes in the United States tend to be more compliance-oriented and are even legalistic, because the laws in the United States tend to leave more business matters to the private sector. They also address the significant risk of litigation. Codes in the European Union tend to be more focused on social responsibility.

ii) Compliance with Industry Standards

An RBE is often a member of an industry as well as a community. Owners and managers take into account industry-specific issues and standards and procedures. In doing so, they should strive to achieve the highest standards of compliance in their industry. Improved industry standards increase transparency and trust in the marketplace, and they enhance the reputation of the industry as a whole.

iii) Protection of the Environment

A code of conduct should address the enterprise's standards, procedures, and expectations regarding the environment. Governments, local communities, NGOs, and international institutions are increasingly using their influence to promote sound environmental practices by business.

A code should include a statement that the enterprise will abide by both local and international laws and regulations designed to protect the environment. It should address how the business balances production objectives with environmental protection in general.

An example of the flow from core values regarding the environment through a basic principle and basic policies to principal activities is set forth in the Japanese NTT Group ethical code of environmental issues.

iv) Respect for Cultural Norms

A code of conduct should demonstrate respect for the cultural norms of the society in which the enterprise operates—especially if it is a transnational enterprise. Employees and agents bring their beliefs, values, and cultural norms to the job. Each society has cultural practices that are unique, including practice of religion, gender relations, and power relationships in the workplace. Implementing and enforcing a code of conduct that does not take these factors into consideration may be seen as unfair and may lead to confusion and frustration.

A number of responsible business conduct issues are unusually culturally sensitive: dealing with conflicts of interest, accepting and giving gifts and gratuities, making facilitation payments, hiring relatives and friends, seeking advice, and reporting misconduct.

A best practice for dealing with these cultural nuances is to require regional divisions of an enterprise to formulate local policies and to submit them for approval. Provided that the local policy reflects the spirit of the general policy and is applied consistently, regional policies can be effective ways to address cultural differences.

v) Guidelines for Developing a Code

The process for developing a code of conduct is as important as the code itself. Engaging stakeholders, demonstrating management commitment, and honouring core beliefs will lead to a clear statement of what the enterprise values.

At the end of the process, the code must be comprehensive enough to give guidance on all important matters to employees and agents. It must describe external stakeholder expectations well enough that they will recognise the enterprise as a contributing member of the community.

One noted author in this field, W. Michael Hoffman, encourages drafters to be particularly concerned with the tone of the code. He recounts how he was once asked to review a code titled "Our Responsibilities." Though he thought it was a good title, "every rule that followed began with 'it is your responsibility to... '" He suggested changing every "your" to "our" to convey the sense that the rules applied to everyone in the company.

Style for a code also depends on the needs and culture of the enterprise. There are many fine examples on the Internet.

i) WMC Resources Ltd., an Australian global mining company, has a very straightforward, colourful, animated code of conduct.

ii) NTT Group, a Japanese telecommunications company, has a detailed environmental code as part of its "Environmental Report 2002."

iii) Guardsmark LLC, a medium sized U.S. firm, has a short code of conduct that lays out principles organized by values and major topics.

iv) HCA Inc., a large U.S. health care company, has a comprehensive code of conduct, as well as policies and procedures for implementing its ethics, compliance, and corporate responsibility program.

v) United Technologies Corporation, a large, global manufacturing firm, has a code of ethics translated into 27 languages, which describes multiple means for an employee or agent to seek advice or report concerns, including regional and headquarters ombudsman offices.

vi) Aspirational versus Obligatory Provisions

Some authors distinguish between code provisions that are aspirational and those that are obligatory. Aspirational provisions are said to be ones that employees and agents are to strive for but for which they will not be held accountable.

An enterprise's standards, procedures, and expectations are intended to guide employees and agents in dealing with real-life issues. If the underlying standard is to apply good judgment, therefore, we are reluctant to say that any standard worth putting in a code of conduct is purely aspirational. The better view is that if a provision is worth putting in a code, then it should be followed.

For the most specific standards—rules—good judgment seldom leads one to violate a rule. When rules are violated, punishment is appropriate since a clear intention to violate rules exists. Although the employee may not be punished as such, failure to use good judgment should not be tolerated.

vii) Adaptations, Updates, and Improvements to the Code

Though a code of conduct is a fundamental document, it is not static. To be effective, it must anticipate the guidance that employees and agents will need to deal appropriately with the challenges they face. Laws and regulations change. Stakeholder expectations change as well. Through commerce with enterprises from different markets, businesses become exposed to new values and beliefs that can affect the way employees view the enterprise and markets.

An RBE should plan in the code itself to monitor closely changes in its relevant context, organisational culture, and stakeholder expectations and to adapt, update, and improve the code accordingly. The RBE must be able to react quickly to changes that affect the enterprise, its markets, and its communities.

viii) Code Formats

Most codes apply one or more of three basic formats:

i) *Compliance Codes*: Specific statements giving guidance and prohibiting certain kinds of conduct;

ii) *Corporate Credos*: Broad general statements of corporate commitments to constituencies, values, and objectives; and

iii) *Management Philosophy Statements*: Formal enunciations of the company or CEO's way of doing business.

An Australian author further distinguishes the formats and objectives of corporate codes of ethics as being of three types:

i) *Codes of ethics*: Statements of the values and principles that define the purpose of an organisation,

ii) *Codes of practice*: Which guide and direct decision–making, and

iii) *Codes of conduct or behaviour*: Which prescribe or proscribe certain behaviour.

Responsible Business Conduct Policies

Once a set of guiding principles, a code of conduct, or both are developed, the process of establishing adequate standards is not complete. To keep these defining documents relatively concise, enterprises typically publish much of the detail that surrounds specific offices or functions, such as internal audit or government contracting, as policies or procedures. An RBE also addresses specific risk areas and opportunities to enhance its reputation or add value to the community.

Effective business ethics programs are designed specifically for the day-to-day challenges of the individual enterprise, its management styles, and its organisational culture. These policies include the following:

1) Policy and procedure development
2) Internal handling of ethics-line calls
3) Self-reporting of violations of certain laws and regulations
4) Business courtesies to potential referral sources
5) Business entertainment

6) Vendor-promotional training
7) Approval of gifts in recognition of volunteer efforts
8) Ethics and compliance officer
9) Code of conduct distribution and training
10) Records management
11) Ethics and compliance program contracts
12) Ethics and compliance office quarterly reports
13) Training for senior management
14) Reportable events

There is no set format for issuing policy and procedures.

Typical Code of Conduct Provisions

The best way to think about what standards, procedures, and expectations to put in a code of conduct is to try to anticipate, from the points of view of stakeholders, the tough decisions that employees and agents might face. With this approach in mind, consider including the items described below.

Introductory Materials

What materials should be included? And why? Introductory materials are highly dependent on the situation, needs, and culture of the enterprise.

An advisable provision to include is a disclaimer. For example, Motorola Corporation avoids creating unrealistic expectations—and unintended liabilities—by placing a disclaimer at the beginning of its code.

Owners

What relationships and responsibilities to its owners should the enterprise assume? And why? Consider the following:

i) Maximising shareholder value
ii) Minimising business risk

iii) Using business resources prudently
iv) Engaging in legal and ethical behaviour
v) Preventing insider trading
vi) Being responsible to community and environment

Customers or Consumers

What relationship and responsibilities to its customers should the enterprise assume? And why? Here are some examples:

1) Providing quality, safe goods and services
2) Representing products or services
3) Communicating clearly so that there is no misunderstanding
4) Protecting confidential information
5) Preventing bribes and kickbacks
6) Regulating gifts and entertainment
7) Including government customer provisions
8) Including foreign government customer provisions
9) Ensuring accurate billing procedures
10) Safeguarding property of others
11) Preventing the disparagement of competitors
12) Ensuring fair competition
13) Acquiring marketing data properly and legally

Employees and the Enterprise

What relationships and responsibilities to its employees should an enterprise assume? What do the employees owe the enterprise? And why? Issues include these:

1) Promoting respect for one another
2) Promoting equal opportunity and anti–harassment
3) Creating a hassle free environment
4) Respecting right to privacy
5) Promoting workplace health and safety

6) Maintaining skills and qualifications
7) Preventing substance abuse
8) Preventing workplace violence
9) Regulating use of company funds
10) Regulating company e-mail and computer use
11) Preventing conflicts of interest
12) Regulating outside business activities
13) Regulating gifts and entertainment
14) Regulating collective bargaining
15) Promoting human rights
16) Excluding child labour
17) Promoting business with the company
18) Regulating employment outside the company
19) Encouraging self-development and lifelong learning
20) Regulating the hire of closely related people
21) Ensuring accurate books and records
21) Retaining records

Partners, Suppliers, and Service Providers

What relationship and responsibilities to its partners, suppliers, and service providers should the enterprise assume? And why? Consider these issues:

i) Treating all suppliers fairly
ii) Regulating the acceptance or offer of gifts and gratuities
iii) Respecting intellectual property of others
iv) Protecting proprietary data of others
v) Using software for its intended purposes
vi) Requiring consultants and suppliers to act legally and ethically

Competitors

What do we owe the competitors? And why? Issues include:

i) Dealing fairly with competitors
ii) Winning on product and service merits
iii) Discouraging comparisons with and disparagement of competitors
iv) Prohibiting inducement of others to break binding contracts with competitors
v) Discouraging the discussion of pricing, costing, marketing, or product plans with competition
vi) Prohibiting illegal or unethical methods to gather competitive information
vii) Preventing unfair competition (antitrust)
viii) Promoting adherence to principles of free competition

Community, Government, and the Environment

What relationship and responsibilities to its communities, governments, and the environment should the enterprise assume? And why?

1) Obeying both the letter and the spirit of law
2) Promoting good competitor relations
3) Complying with local laws and customs
4) Promoting anticorruption practices
5) Excluding foreign corrupt practices
6) Regulating political contributions
7) Regulating political activity
8) Including indigenous peoples
9) Promoting sustainable development
10) Complying with anti–money laundering measures
11) Complying with antiboycott laws
12) Complying with import–export laws
13) Voluntarily disclosing violations
14) Cooperating with authorities
15) Promoting charitable contributions

16) Encouraging employee volunteer work
17) Protecting the environment

Business Ethics Program

A business ethic program should cover these issues:

1) Ethics and compliance structure and systems
2) Responsibility of managers and supervisors
3) Need to avoid even the appearance of impropriety
4) Monitoring and auditing practices
5) Employees' duty to report violations
6) Failure to comply
7) Failure to detect misconduct
8) Methods to seek advice and report misconduct
9) Policy concerning false reports
10) Enterprise response to reports
11) Policy for customer, supplier, and contact agents
12) Confidentiality and anonymity policy
13) Non–retaliation policy
14) Policy for employee misconduct
15) Policy for rewarding ethical behaviour
16) Records retention
17) Media contact
18) Individual accountability
19) Obligation to sign acknowledgment

Business Ethics Program Resources

Resources may include these:

i) Ethical decision-making model
ii) Case studies and examples
iii) Telephone contact numbers

Design, Review, and Approval Process

The code and supporting policies will not be finally approved until all standards, procedures, and expectations as well as implementing policies and infrastructure have been designed and approved.

REFERENCES

Aristotle (1987). *Nicomachean Ethics*. New York, Prometheus Books

Program, G. G. (2004). *Business Ethics: A manual for managing a responsible business enterprise in emerging market economies*. Washington DC, Good Governance Program, US Department of Commerce.

Solomon, R. (1999). *Business ethics and virtue. A Companion to Business Ethics*. R. Frederick. Oxford, Blackwell: 30–37.

Samuels, W., J (1977). *Ideology in Economics Modern Economic Thought*. S. Weintraub. Oxford, Blackwell: 467–484.

8

Business Ethics Communications

Communication in the responsible business enterprise (RBE) is mutual—that is, owners and managers strive to make sure employees and agents understand their standards, procedures, and expectations, and owners, managers, supervisors, workers, and agents alike have the information they need when they need it.

Communicating and Providing Feedback

For an enterprise to be responsible, all stakeholders must have a complete understanding of their roles and responsibilities in the workings of its business ethics infrastructure. Moreover, managers must know whether the enterprise's standards, procedures, and expectations are adequate to meet the reasonable expectations of its stakeholders. Owners and managers ask themselves two fundamental questions:

i) How can we most effectively communicate the standards and procedures and foster reasonable expectations among our stakeholders?

ii) How can we know that our members follow our standards and that reasonable stakeholder expectations are met?

A primary cultural characteristic of an enterprise is the extent to which knowledge is shared. Communication within an RBE is not top-down but instead flows in all directions. How the elements of a business ethics program are communicated is an integral part of the program itself. The manner in which owners and managers communicate the value they place in the program through the choices they make, the things they say, and what they do or fail to do will define the program for most other stakeholders.

Developing a Communications Program

For owners and managers to communicate about responsible business conduct, they must be working from a communications program that delivers a clear and consistent message of what it means for the enterprise to be responsible.

Formal communications are the most obvious aspect: program announcements, company newsletters, new employee orientation, training programs, posters, annual and social responsibility reports, speeches, and meetings. Owners and managers must be alert to both forms of communication. If formal communications tell one story while informal communications tell another, stakeholders often become frustrated and cynical.

In planning the communications program, owners and managers need to identify their stakeholders and prioritise communication efforts among them. They must consider how best to reach particular stakeholders.

The communications program also needs to address how to solicit and respond to feedback from employees and other stakeholders. Feedback helps the enterprise track whether its standards and procedures are known and followed.

i) Know the Audience

For the RBE, the target audience includes all stakeholders. Stakeholders and their interests are identified through the processes of scanning the relevant context and organisational culture described. Through these processes, owners and managers gain a firm understanding of what is required of the enterprise for its business ethics program to be effective.

Stakeholders, whether internal or external, often have widely differing perspectives on enterprise standards, procedures, and expectations.

Internal stakeholders can be categorised in terms of their interest in ethics:

i) Some employees are *ethical enthusiasts:* These employees hold views on corporate responsibility that are strong enough to influence their choice of employer.

ii) Others are *ethically committed*: These employees have adopted enterprise standards, procedures, and expectations in principle but still require support. They need to be assured that their choices and actions will meet the enterprise's expectations.

iii) Other employees are *ethically unaware*: These employees are not aware of—or have not yet embraced—these standards, procedures, and expectations and need to be educated about them, employees' individual roles and responsibilities, and the business ethics infrastructure built to ensure that standards, procedures, and expectations are honoured.

iv) Still other employees are *ethically challenged*: They have quietly rejected enterprise standards and procedures because they make lucrative "business as usual" more difficult. These people need to be advised that:

   a) The enterprise is dedicated to its standards, procedures, and expectations and

   b) Deviation from them will not be tolerated. Often, these people will self–select themselves out of the enterprise when they come to appreciate that owners and managers are genuinely committed.

Much the same categorisation can be made of external stakeholders. The enterprise message needs to resonate with certain external stakeholders, who can be thought of as potential allies. Some stakeholder advocacy groups, for example, will work cooperatively with an RBE to help it better understand the impact of its activities on others, provided they are convinced that the enterprise is interested in finding mutually satisfactory solutions.

Other stakeholders are well intentioned but hostile to an enterprise because they do not understand its purpose or the challenges facing it. The conflict revolved around which method of disposal would cause the least environmental damage. Greenpeace was unwilling to consider any method other than land decommissioning. Royal Dutch/Shell had to make the scientific case for its method of disposal and consider "social, ethical, aesthetic, legal and economic factors ... in addition to the scientific evidence."

Finally, some external stakeholders are hostile to capitalism in general. Others object to specific business practices of a particular enterprise. In Islamic countries, for example, producing pork products or alcohol is unacceptable. Some stakeholder groups remain suspicious of Nestlé for marketing infant formula in impoverished countries that did not have the hygiene capabilities and literacy to use the product properly. Other stakeholder groups will never accept tobacco manufacturers or defense contractors as responsible businesses. For an enterprise to engage such stakeholders, an effective communications program must address their concerns as directly as possible, without sacrificing core beliefs.

ii) Assess the Needs

Before designing a communications program, owners and managers must conduct a needs analysis to find out what stakeholders need to know. In general, a need to communicate enterprise standards, procedures, and expectations to employees and agents is clear.

Owners and managers need to know much more than the target audiences to design an effective communications program. Management should use a number of standard assessment tools such as interviews, focus groups, surveys, document review, and direct observation to ask the following questions:

i) What kinds of responsible business conduct issues do employees and other stakeholders face or are they concerned about?

ii) What do employees and other stakeholders need to know to be able to fulfill their roles and responsibilities and have reasonable expectations of the enterprise?

iii) How do employees and other stakeholders learn what is expected of them and what they can expect?

iv) What communications methods are available to the enterprise to reach specific stakeholders?

v) What are the criteria by which successful communications will be evaluated?

Using RBE Worksheet 9 in conjunction with other worksheets, such as RBE Worksheet 2 and RBE Worksheet 4, will help management determine *what* needs to be communicated to *whom* and *how*. With the information obtained, a working group can develop a plan to design a comprehensive communications program.

Typically, the most important stakeholders to reach will be customers, employees, and agents. Next in priority may be financial stakeholders, such as owners and investors, and then, specific stakeholder advocacy groups. Management needs to conduct this analysis carefully to ensure that its message about standards, procedures, and expectations is communicated as effectively and efficiently as possible.

The product of this needs analysis should be a summary report describing the program situation, target audiences, objectives, program resources and constraints, and expected outcomes.

Communicating Standards, Procedures, and Expectations

Standards, procedures, and expectations of responsible business conduct should be communicated through as many means as are likely to be well received by the target audience. Some means are dictated by law, such as annual reports to shareholders or environmental impact assessments to government agencies.

An important part of any communications program is training, education, and development. For the RBE, training must be comprehensive. For an enterprise to be responsible as a whole, each of its employees and agents must have the skills, knowledge, understanding, and attitudes necessary to work together to achieve enterprise goals and objectives.

i) Promoting the Program through Management Speeches

There is no doubt that when owners and managers speak employees and other stakeholders listen—at least to some degree. Employees and other stakeholders are also alert to what is *not* said, as much (or more) than what is said. Owners and managers need to be particularly alert to the risk of mentioning enterprise core beliefs or the business ethics program only on special occasions. It escaped few employees that, while he lauded the program on the day set aside to honour it, he never referred to, or inquired after, it at any other time. Especially when introducing a business ethics program, managers need to accept that their message may be greeted skeptically.

ii) Distributing Statements, Codes, Standards, Procedures, and Expectations

As stressed in earlier that establish responsible business conduct standards, procedures, and expectations are only the start of a business ethics program. To the extent employees and other stakeholders were formally involved in writing the basic documents setting forth guidance and establishing expectations, the communications process has begun.

Distributing copies of the responsible business conduct standards, procedures, and expectations to each employee and agent, and requiring them to acknowledge receipt, is a major step. For the newly hired in an enterprise, the documents establishing standards, procedures, and expectations for responsible business conduct should be among the first matters addressed during orientation. Some enterprises discuss their core beliefs as early as the recruiting process. Some companies distribute wallet–size cards with enterprise core beliefs and business ethics contact information to all employees. Others put such information on the back of employee identification cards.

iii) Posting Summaries or Lists of Principles

A cost–effective means of reinforcing the message of responsible business conduct is to post enterprise core beliefs in lobbies, meeting rooms, and work spaces, as well as on bulletin boards. When one enterprise was responding to a responsible business conduct crisis, a manager began each meeting by reciting the enterprise business principles or core values. Posting is a means of communicating, but owners, managers, and supervisors need to make sure the message is actually understood.

iv) Posting on a Web Site

Increasingly, standards, procedures, and expectations for responsible business conduct are posted on the enterprise Web site or intranet. This information usually includes the enterprise core beliefs, statement of business principles, and annual report.

v) Publishing Articles and Newsletters

Articles or columns about responsible business conduct can be placed regularly in enterprise publications. In larger enterprises, the business ethics program may have its own newsletter. Whatever the medium, articles may address issues of particular concern to management.

A particularly sensitive question is how to address incidents that have led to the disciplining of an employee. There is no better way to demonstrate management's commitment to responsible business conduct standards, procedures, and expectations than to disclose publicly how managers dealt with a difficult situation—particularly when the matter involved a senior executive.

While recognising the value in addressing real–life issues and describing real–life responses, managers must consider the privacy rights of the employee before publishing details of the incident. If the enterprise is small enough, or the event notorious enough, however, the employee's identity may be clear to all employees. The same may also be true when an employee is rewarded for some ethically exemplary decision or action. In many organisational cultures, individual rewards or rewards for reporting concerns about another member of the group would degrade the harmony of the group itself.

vi) Making Ethics Brochures Readily Available

Where there are matters of particular concern to management, employees and agents may be given brochures to address them. Among many others, topics may include dealing with conflicts of interest, accepting or declining gifts and gratuities, meeting stakeholder expectations, and seeking advice and reporting concerns.

Creating a Training Program

Making speeches and distributing written materials are necessary elements of getting the message out, but they are not enough. All employees—from senior managers to workers—need time on the job to review responsible business standards, procedures, and expectations; to explore issues of responsible business conduct.

Designing a training program requires the same attention to objectives and outcomes as does the design of the business ethics program as a whole. It requires attention to the situation, resources available, activities and participants, target audiences, outputs, and expected outcomes. In short, it is not clear to all what success looks like.

i) Demonstrating Management Commitment

Few decisions symbolise management's commitment to its business ethics program more than devoting time, on a regular basis, to training in responsible business conduct. Beyond the skills, knowledge, and understanding developed through such training, the mere fact that management dedicates valuable employee time to such training goes a long way toward demonstrating that it is serious about its standards, procedures, and expectations becoming part of the organisational culture.

Rescheduling busy day–to–day operations to accommodate regular employee training also conveys an important message from managers and supervisors to their workers.

ii) Reinforcing Core Beliefs and Organisational Culture

Training should be designed as an essential link between the enterprise's core beliefs, the business ethics program, and the expected program outcomes.

The training program should reflect the organisational culture of the enterprise. The enterprise needs to project the expected behaviour through the training program. Training should also contribute to the expected outcomes of the business ethics program. Where employees are not used to being asked how they would address important issues, let alone raise them, training will need to demonstrate how it is done—and engage the employees as their comfort level increases.

iii) Designing the Program

Training program objectives depend on relevant context,

organisational culture, goals and objectives, and expected outcomes for the business ethics program as a whole. Designing the training program begins with the summary report of the communications needs assessment. The training program should be based on enterprise core beliefs.

At a minimum, training sessions should require employees to become familiar with applicable laws and regulations, as well as with the enterprise's procedures for reporting and investigating concerns about responsible business conduct. It should include an examination of the criteria for ethical decision–making.

All participants should leave the training program confident that they know what the enterprise expects of them and what they can expect from the enterprise in turn. They should be able to recognise issues of responsible business conduct and have the confidence—and courage—to make the right decision, explain that decision to the appropriate people, and act accordingly. They should understand how the business ethics program relates to strategic issues for the RBE as a whole.

For a training program to contribute to expected outcomes, it requires a heavy emphasis on dialogue and decision-making about issues of responsible business conduct. Beyond developing listening and feedback skills and good judgment in enterprise members, the training program must convey managements sincere desire to know whether its standards and procedures are being followed and whether its stakeholder expectations are being met. This task requires not only encouraging individuals who are inclined to come forward but also explaining to those who do not why their silence is detrimental to enterprise performance.

A typical expected outcome is that employees and agents will use good judgment in addressing issues of responsible business conduct. At a minimum, management might provide a decision–making process that, in a specific incident, enables its employees and agents

i) To define the issues of ethics, compliance, and responsibility

ii) To demonstrate a grasp of all relevant and material facts, including the stakeholders involved and their interests

iii) To point to the applicable standards, procedures, and expectations, including decrees, laws, and regulations

iv) To describe the range of options available

v) To explain why, based on these considerations, they made a particular choice or acted in a particular manner

Many ethics and policy decision-making models are available on the Internet. They range from simple, five-step models to multiphase frame works that include decision criteria. The better models are based on well-developed skills in critical thinking. Trainers can introduce the process through lecture and then break the participants into small groups to apply it in a case study.

A long-term expected program outcome should be an organisational culture in which owners and managers have the information they need to make intelligent decisions for the enterprise.

Participants must also leave training firmly convinced that, should they make a mistake, they will not be punished if they can demonstrate that they followed the enterprise decision-making process. Employees or agents should not be punished for making a mistake if they can demonstrate that they:

i) Recognised the issue

ii) Had a reasonable grasp of the relevant facts

iii) Considered enterprise standards, procedures, and expectations

iv) Explored the range of options available

v) Could justify the choice they made or action they took

Delivering the Training Program

A number of principles characterise effective training programs on responsible business conduct. First, a program should project the core beliefs of the enterprise—not just teach them. Second, owners and managers should be involved in the training in significant, visible ways. Third, the program should recognise the personal values of individual stakeholders but not rely on them. Fourth, the program should be comprehensive, not limited to specific training in responsible business conduct. Finally, it should include action planning and follow-up to reinforce the lessons learned.

i) Reflecting Core Beliefs

Where expected program objectives include issue recognition, dialogue, and ethical decision–making, the training program should develop those skills and provide the knowledge necessary to apply them.

In developing those skills and passing on this knowledge, the program needs to project the core beliefs of the enterprise and the expected program outcomes. It is one thing to discuss rules governing bribery and corruption because they are in the code of conduct. It is another thing to tell sto ies about how those rules are applied in practice.

ii) Involving Owners and Managers

Because all training must reflect the relevant context and organisational culture of the enterprise, the precise way to involve owners and managers cannot be specified. A key requirement is that stakeholders, especially employees, believe that management fully supports the training.

Management involvement takes many forms. Some enterprises use cascade training, in which the CEO trains his or her direct subordinates. This method has the advantage of actively involving managers, which tends to demonstrate commitment. A disadvantage may be that the presence of managers may stifle active involvement of the employees when candid discussion of issues is in order or when the culture of the enterprise is to remain silent on important issues.

Another option is a video of the CEO introducing the training by declaring his or her personal commitment to the training program.

iii) Recognising Personal Values

One of the controversies surrounding training in responsible business conduct is whether one can—or should—teach ethics to adults. It is unlikely that ethics training will change the outlook of most employees. But the purpose of business ethics training is not so much to change adults as it is to support them, admonish them, or reinforce their understanding of management's commitment to enforcing its standards, procedures, and expectations.

Trainers can be confident that what adults bring with them to the enterprise does not include knowledge of enterprise standards, procedures, and expectations. For some employees and agents, no amount of training is going to change them.

For the training to be effective, it must appeal to what motivates the participants. The ideal situation permits an appeal to a participant's sense of community. Where participants feel that they share a purpose, values, and a vision of a desired future, trainers may stress responsibilities to stakeholders. But more often, participants respond to a sense of urgency.

One cost-effective way of creating a sense of urgency is to develop a "parade of horribles" by collecting headlines of powerful enterprises and individuals who have been prosecuted or held liable for misconduct. "The Bigger They Are, the Harder They Fall," said the headline of one recent working paper, which estimated that "the loss of confidence following the collapse of Enron and WorldCom will cost the U.S. economy $37 billion to $42 billion" in reduced gross domestic product. Few responsible business conduct trainers now miss an opportunity to refer to Enron to demonstrate what can happen if managers act irresponsibly—what has come to be known as the "Enron Effect."

iv) Making Training Comprehensive

Training should take place at all levels of the enterprise. From senior managers and owners to workers on the shop floor, every employee and agent should receive training in responsible business conduct specific to his or her level of responsibility. All employees and agents should review enterprise core beliefs, standards, procedures, and expectations, including policies relating to their individual responsibilities.

Managers and supervisors need additional training to reflect their roles and responsibilities as integral parts of the business ethics program. In particular, they must understand that enterprise standards, procedures, and expectations are never to be violated to meet individual and enterprise performance objectives. They must fully appreciate their roles and responsibilities in nurturing an organisational culture in which employees and agents can seek advice and report concerns so that management has the information it needs to guide the enterprise.

Agents, including consultants, sales agents, brokers, partners, franchises, and closely allied suppliers and service providers, should be exposed to the enterprise core beliefs; applicable standards, procedures, and expectations; and specific policies relating to their roles and responsibilities.

Training should address pursuing the enterprise's purpose and meeting stakeholder expectations. A training program begins with basic employee recruiting materials and procedures, and never truly ends.

For example, concerns such as customer service, quality management, fair dealing with suppliers and service providers, environmental protection, proper relationships with government officials, and individual responsibility for developing a healthy workplace require attention to issues far beyond business ethics. Although basic training in workplace skills is not specifically training in responsible business conduct, ensuring that employees and agents have the requisite skills, knowledge, understanding, and attitudes to pursue the enterprise's purpose and meet reasonable stakeholder expectations *is* responsible business conduct. Preaching a core value of customer service when employees know they do not have the ability to provide it will build, at best, frustration and cynicism.

v) Incorporating Action Planning and Action Learning

One way to make training meaningful is to have participants, individually or as members of a team, develop an action plan for the next three to six months based on what they learned. For senior employees, this action plan may reflect an assessment that some aspects of an enterprise's business ethics program require more support in practice. Another might be a need to develop a division policy on waste water disposal.

Copies of these action plans should be retained by the business ethics officer or another appropriate officer. Follow–up questionnaires requesting progress reports should be sent regularly. Tracking progress on action plans can give indirect feedback or function as a performance evaluation item. An important way to demonstrate management commitment is to include participation in the training and action planning as express elements of performance evaluation.

The Modes of Training

The training program should use all modes appropriate to the organisational culture and stakeholder needs. In general, training should be as interactive, realistic, and relevant to day–to–day jobs as possible. In a recent study, one researcher found that European "training objectives typically include illumination of the company's and individual's values while in the United States the emphasis is on increasing knowledge of company standards and/or the law." The level of difficulty should challenge but not overwhelm participants.

Some modes of training that enterprises may consider include:

i) *Lectures and presentations:* The classic method that adults are familiar with from their school days, lectures are the most effective way to reach a number of people with fairly straightforward information. In the initial rollout of a code, for example, lectures may be the most effective mode of explaining where the code fits into business performance.

ii) *Case studies and scenarios:* After participants understand the purpose of the training and the resources available, issues of responsible business conduct can be effectively introduced through the study and analysis of cases that have actually occurred to the enterprise or to other similarly situated enterprises. Trainers might also develop their own scenarios to raise a number of issues. Case studies and scenarios help develop dialogue and decision–making skills.

iii) *Ethics games:* Many larger enterprises, including Citigroup, Lockheed Martin, and Boeing, have developed games to raise awareness of issues of ethics, compliance, and social responsibility; to develop good reasoning skills and judgment; to stimulate dialogue; and to demonstrate management commitment. In general, the games involve dividing employees into small teams and placing before them a situation that raises a discrete issue of ethics, compliance, or social responsibility.

iv) *Other modes:* Many companies are now offering quite sophisticated Web based training. This mode may be relatively cost-effective. Videos and self–paced studies may be purchased off the shelf and may expose participants to the basics.

Updating and Modifying the Training Program

The training program should be modified over time to ensure that its content contributes to pursuit of the enterprise's purpose and helps meet reasonable stakeholder expectations. Also, it should be reviewed to ensure that the delivery methods are the most effective available.

Training provides useful feedback to managers on the ways in which the business ethics program is being received. It helps uncover sensitive areas such as insufficient guidance for employees or unreasonable stakeholder expectations, legal issues, unfair treatment of employees, and difficult working conditions. Feedback might reveal that trainers focus on issues that do not reflect the real-life concerns of the participants. It might also show that the sessions need more trainer–trainee interaction or that the materials are dull and do not encourage interaction.

There are several methods for collecting feedback from training programs. Traditionally, training administrators ask trainees to fill out an evaluation form asking whether they found the training useful and what, if anything, they learned. At the end of the training, administrators should ask participants questions such as:

i) How would you rate the overall effectiveness of the training?

ii) Were the materials helpful and relevant?

iii) Were the right issues discussed?

iv) What other topics would you like to discuss in the next training session?

Training administrators might also ask participants to take quizzes before, during, and after the training to determine what they learned.

Managing Training Administration

Owners and managers demonstrate their commitment to the business ethics program by managing the training program well. Good management requires that adequate time be allocated to training, that training records be well maintained, and that training participation be an element of performance evaluation.

Generally, three to four hours of training per employee, at a minimum, is required to roll out a new business ethics program. In the United States, it is common for all employees and agents to be required to attend the training. In Europe, training tends to be more targeted and to take place at higher management levels. Additional training should be provided for people in sensitive positions, such as government contracting, sales and marketing, and human resources. Good records management requires that training administrators record participation in training.

IMPORTANCE OF FEEDBACK

Few stakeholders of an enterprise would disagree with the proposition that owners and managers have legitimate needs for information about compliance with its standards, procedures, and expectations.

The abiding issue for a business ethics program is how to garner this information through processes that are consistent with the enterprise's core beliefs. The ideal form is free–flowing communication between owners and managers, employees and agents, and other stakeholders about all the matters needed for the enterprise to meet the reasonable expectations of its stakeholders effectively and efficiently. Often, however, either mechanisms to accommodate free–flowing communication are not readily available or there is not enough trust between stakeholders for such communication to take place.

In general, owners and managers use five methods to track what is going on in the enterprise:

i) Monitoring ongoing operations
ii) Auditing books, records, and process documentation
iii) Responding to employees and agents seeking advice and reporting concerns
iv) Investigating incidents and reports
v) Engaging stakeholders

All these methods require infrastructure. Engaging external stakeholders is not as well defined as the other methods, but enterprises have found a few techniques, such as stakeholder surveys, to be valuable.

Monitoring

Monitoring enterprise performance is an essential management task. An RBE plans its work by assigning individual and group responsibility. It sets performance expectations for individuals and groups to guide their efforts toward achieving the enterprise's goals and objectives. Employees and agents are held accountable as individuals and groups for achieving assigned objectives while following the enterprise's standards, procedures, and expectations.

In an RBE, processes and projects may be monitored continually. Good monitoring requires consistently measuring performance and providing ongoing feedback to employees and agents as to how well their performance complies with enterprise standards and procedures and meets stakeholder expectations.

The best operational example is the total quality management process, whereby individuals and teams set performance standards, continually collect data, and use quality tools to measure performance and analyse the data to resolve problems and improve processes.

Issues of responsible business conduct may be approached in a similar manner. Where risks have been identified, such as conflicts of interest, fraudulent consumer transactions, inaccurate books and records or expense accounting, or bribes and corruption, an RBE establishes structures and systems to monitor performance on a regular basis. It does not wait for reports of misconduct. Other forms of monitoring are performance evaluations and exit interviews.

Auditing

Whereas monitoring is an aspect of good management practice for all managers and supervisors, auditing is a more formal process. It is a review of employee or agent performance by an independent agent. This independent agent may be either internal or external to the enterprise, but it is not a part of the enterprise's operational management.

Internal audit serves as the primary means by which owners and managers review and evaluate the enterprise's internal control structure.

More recently, the traditional focus has expanded to include reviewing the systems established to ensure compliance with an enterprise's standards, procedures, and expectations. They may be done on a regular basis or in response to specific reports or concerns.

Employees Seeking Advice and Reporting Concerns

Among the surest sources of information about what is going on in an enterprise—especially behaviour that violates enterprise core beliefs, standards, procedures, and expectations—are employees and agents. Most employees and agents recognise management's legitimate need for such information, if the enterprise is to meet the reasonable expectations of its stakeholders.

Reporting concerns about the business conduct of co-workers is hard for most employees. Indeed, research suggests that substantial numbers of employees, even in developed economies, are extremely reluctant to report their concerns. Many put loyalty to friends and colleagues above loyalty to the enterprise.

A business ethics program helps employees and agents understand why it is important that they communicate their concerns to management, how they should report their concerns, and why it is safe to do so.

Under a business ethics program, employees and agents are more sensitive to the types of behaviour that constitute misconduct or illegality. They are more likely to view reporting misconduct as one of their obligations to the enterprise, their fellow employees, and enterprise stakeholders.

In an organisational culture that encourages dialogue, questions, and delivery of bad news, employees find it easier to confront issues of responsible business conduct, to seek advice and report concerns, and to make ethical decisions. In many enterprises, however, employees are uncomfortable with coming forward, especially to report their concerns involving other employees. Owners and managers need to make the case for coming forward in terms that resonate with their employees.

i) Reporting Violations

Ideally, owners, managers, and supervisors maintain an open–door policy for employees and agents who have concerns that involve responsible business conduct. Often, however, employees and agents are reluctant to bring "bad news" to managers and supervisors.

Suggestion boxes, help–lines, and whistle–blowing protection all facilitate reporting of questionable conduct. Reports may also be received from individuals who come to the business ethics office and register a concern. The identity of reporters should be kept confidential, and sources should not be held liable, discriminated against, or harassed for reporting their concerns.

Once the business ethics officer receives a report, it is important that the enterprise follow through. The officer should

i) Record the reported concern

ii) Evaluate the concern and develop an action plan for dealing with it

iii) Initiate or coordinate an investigation or inquiry, if appropriate

iv) Take appropriate action on findings and conclusions

v) Track reported concerns for patterns and trends

vi) Make recommendations based on lessons learned

Critical to the success of the business ethics program is feedback to the reporting source of the steps taken to investigate the matter, what was found, and what corrective steps—if any—were or will be taken.

ii) Protecting Employees and Agents from Retribution

All reporting procedures should be designed to leave reporters free from fear of retribution. Managers, supervisors, and other employees should understand that direct or indirect retribution for voicing a concern or complaint is not to be tolerated. Retribution by either managers or peers discourages others from reporting their concerns.

Occasionally, an employee or other agent reporting concerns may make a mistake or abuse the reporting process and cause an investigation that does not lead to further action. Behaviour that abuses the reporting process will often violate enterprise core beliefs; however, managers should counsel, but not punish, such a reporter.

Maintaining absolute certainty among employees and agents that they can report concerns without fear of retribution is so important that managers should not risk losing that confidence by punishing anyone who used a reporting process. Where trust in management is not the norm, reporting sources may be uncertain about just how safely they can make reports.

Moreover, it is difficult, at best, to prove that a reported concern was an abuse of the process. Even if a case can be made, it may raise significant questions in the minds of potential sources about just how safe the process is. In short, for all the satisfaction owners and managers may retain in being able to punish someone who abuses the process, the cost in terms of employee confidence in the reporting process is too high to pay.

Although the individual should not be punished to preserve confidence in the business ethics program, other steps can be taken to limit harm to other individuals or to the enterprise. The abusing person or the victim may be reassigned, for example.

iii) Using a Help-Line

A help–line is a dedicated telephone line that gives employees and agents direct access to the business ethics officer. It should be free of charge to the caller. The number should be widely distributed; everyone should have access to the number. If the enterprise uses an answering machine for the number after normal business hours, the machine should be placed in a private, secure location.

A help–line may be operated by a commercial service with instructions from the enterprise.

iv) Maintaining Confidentiality and Security

It is difficult for an employee or agent to choose fidelity to enterprise standards, procedures, and expectations over loyalty to his or her friends or colleagues. When an employee or agent decides to report concerns, he or she must believe that it is the right thing to do.

An emerging best practice is to establish a policy authorising certain business ethics personnel to promise reporting employees and agents that their identities and information will remain confidential.

Whether they can make a promise of confidentiality that courts of law will respect, known as a *privileged communication*, depends on the laws of the jurisdiction.

v) Distinguishing between Ethics and Personnel Issues

Experience with help–lines demonstrates that more than half of all calls will be about personnel matters. Owners and managers will be tempted to require that such callers be directed to call human resources. They should resist this temptation for two reasons. First, in the minds of employees, when managers speak of ethics, they are talking about fairness, so employees see personnel matters as ethics issues. Second, when management rejects a call to the help–line for whatever reason it risks the reputation of the help-line as an effective and safe way for employees and agents to seek advice or report concerns. Other employees will only hear that a fellow employee made a call to the help-line and was rejected, but not learn management's reasons why, however valid.

In establishing reporting guidelines, however, management must distinguish between matters of responsible business conduct and grievances of union–represented employees.

The Organisational Ombudsman

In a number of large, complex enterprises (LCEs), a specific office, called the *ombudsman*, has been established to advise employees and agents of their rights and duties regarding responsible conduct. In the business enterprise context, the ombudsman is a separate means by which employees and agents can seek advice and report their concerns.

The ombudsman was originally a Scandinavian office created to investigate citizen complaints against governments or otherwise trusted to look after the affairs of others. Position of ombudsman in a business ethics programme has become independent neutral and alternative. *Independent* means the ombudsman is not a part of day–to–day staff or operations management. *Neutral* means it does not function as an advocate for the enterprise or individual. *Alternative* means the ombudsman does not duplicate any other enterprise function, such as investigations. With few exceptio[illegible] the ombudsman is authorised to refer reports of misconduct for investigation only with the express consent of the reporting source.

In some jurisdictions, enterprises can claim that the ombudsman can make an enforceable promise of confidentiality. The enterprise will not be deemed to have notice of the concern until the source registers his or her concerns with the enterprise or authorizes the ombudsman to do so.

Policies and Procedures for Investigations

It is critical to the success of a business ethics program that reported concerns be investigated. Managers may learn of concerns suggesting that a violation of standards, procedures, and expectations has occurred from a variety of sources, including the help–line.

In developing an investigative plan, managers need to consider the laws of the jurisdiction in which they operate. These laws will affect who conducts the investigation and what rights are afforded to the subjects of the investigation. Investigations should always be conducted with a view to possible government prosecution or civil litigation.

Investigations will typically involve document review and witness interviews. Employees should be instructed to cooperate fully with the investigation, including preserving all relevant documents and materials.

External Stakeholder Engagement

Increasingly, non-governmental organisations (NGOs) hold enterprises accountable for unethical behaviour and demand best practices. International institutions are developing policies requiring greater transparency and encouraging official investigations of misconduct. Local communities are less willing to host an enterprise known for corrupt or irresponsible practices.

These trends provide owners and managers with the incentive and opportunity to secure feedback from external stakeholders. Feedback mechanisms include media reviews, stakeholder satisfaction surveys, conferences, and discussion groups. Also important is public perception about how responsible the enterprise is or how consistent its business practices are with its core beliefs.

Meetings with external stakeholders are an effective way to secure feedback. An RBE can sponsor such meetings to demonstrate its initiative and interest. An owner or senior manager should lead the meetings. Local community, government, and NGO representatives may be invited. Questions, comments, and suggestions should be encouraged.

Monitoring media coverage of business is an essential means of securing feedback from the public and making appropriate adjustments to the business ethics program. In recent years, the media have become better informed about how to measure whether leaders of an enterprise are committed to responsible business conduct.

An RBE engages its stakeholders by monitoring, tracking, and reporting its performance in areas of concern to its stakeholders, especially civil society. The reaction of civil society and the media to the enterprise's social responsibility reports is valuable information and invites further dialogue.

It is vital to the welfare of the enterprise and its ability to meet the reasonable expectations of its stakeholders that owners and managers know whether enterprise standards and procedures are being followed and whether reasonable stakeholder expectations are being met. The source of this information, in all cases, is the stakeholders of the enterprise: employees, agents, customers, suppliers, and regulators, to name but a few.

Owners and managers of an RBE should develop a plan to communicate with stakeholders the enterprise's standards, procedures, and expectations. They can do so by answering two fundamental questions:

i) How can we most effectively communicate our standards and procedures and foster reasonable expectations among our stakeholders?

ii) How can we know that our members follow our standards and reasonable stakeholder expectations are met?

To communicate enterprise standards, procedures, and expectations, owners and managers use all manner of vehicles: formal and informal communications; training, education, and development; and stakeholder engagement.

To ensure that management knows what is going on in the enterprise, owners and managers establish various mechanisms, as appropriate to the relevant context and organisational culture: monitoring, auditing, reporting, and stakeholder surveys.

References

Cetina, K. K. and A. Preda, Eds. (2005). *The sociology of financial markets*. Oxford, Oxford University Press.

Grabel, I. (2008). *Global finance and development: false starts, dead ends and social economic alternatives. The Elgar Companion to Social Economics*. J. B. Davis and W. Dolfsma. Cheltenham, Edward Elgar: 496–519.

Groucutt, J., P. Leadley, et al. (2004). *Marketing: essential principles, new realities*. London, Kogan Page.

9

Alignment Practices of Responsible Business Enterprises

Core beliefs, standards, and procedures; reasonable stakeholder expectations; and business ethics infrastructure alone do not make an enterprise a responsible business. Research and experience suggest that the most helpful aspect of a business ethics program may be that it supports management practices that align enterprise strategies and management practices with core beliefs, standards, procedures, infrastructure, and expectations.

A business ethics program is a fundamental aspect of organisational development that provides the foundation for other important aspects of business planning such as a business plan, marketing strategy, investment prospectus, and proposal for a strategic alliance. In all these instances, the enterprise must be able to demonstrate a consistent theme in thought, communication, and action.

i) Mission

ii) Goals and objectives

iii) Strategies, programs, and action plans

iv) Performance measures

v) Decisions and activities

In the case of a business plan, for example, all of the elements lead to an integrated approach to the four components of a business plan:

i) Description of the business,

ii) Marketing plan,

iii) Financial management plan, and

iv) Management plan.

A business plan not based on these elements would be necessarily incomplete.

Three fundamental questions address the alignment practices of an RBE:

i) How can we ensure that we have the right people in the right places while we pursue our purpose as an enterprise?

ii) How can we encourage the employees and agents to follow the standards and procedures?

iii) What do we owe the stakeholders when mistakes, misconduct, or misunderstandings occur that involve our standards and procedures or their reasonable expectations?

Getting the Right People in the Right Places

Having the right people in place allows an enterprise to face a changing world confident that it can succeed, regardless of the pressures its relevant context might present. To accomplish this, management needs to attract the right people, train them properly, position them well, and treat them fairly.

Having Responsible Owners, Managers, and Supervisors

Emphasis on having the right people in the right places begins with owners, managers, and supervisors. Responsible owners and managers need to be people who embrace an RBE's core beliefs. If an RBE's purpose is to be a global energy company, as at Royal Dutch/ Shell, then they are passionate about delivering energy on a global scale. If the enterprise's values are integrity, contribution to society, responsibility to customers and employees, and the unequivocal pursuit of quality and excellence, those values naturally guide everything owners and managers think, say, or do.

Owners, managers, and supervisors set the tone for all that happens— and does not happen—in their enterprise. Employees and agents watch to see if they "pay attention to ethics, take ethics seriously, and care about ethics and values as much as the bottom line," as one recent study confirmed. Over time, their behaviour molds the organisational culture that orders "the way we do things around here," regardless of what the formal documents of the enterprise might say.

Owners, managers, and supervisors are in positions that have authority and require discretion. The decisions they make and the activities they sponsor or condone involve great risk and opportunity for the enterprise.Mistakes might have implications at all four levels of enterprise identity:

i) *Compliance level:* Prosecutors are far more likely to prosecute an enterprises for criminal misconduct if senior managers are involved; they are more likely to find that the organisational culture of the enterprise is a factor, as well.

ii) *Risk management level:* Risk to the enterprise may be dramatically higher if senior managers or those with substantial discretion are involved, often costing into the millions of dollars.

iii) *Reputation enhancement level:* The damage to the reputation of the enterprise, especially when senior managers are involved, may be irreparable. In recent years, for example, enterprises with household names have ceased to exist or are struggling to recover from lapses in responsible business conduct at the level of senior management.

iv) *Value–added level:* An RBE strives to add value to its community while drawing on the resources of the community.

What makes any person a "right person" for a particular enterprise, then, are the responsible criteria of the enterprise itself: its core beliefs, its established standards and procedures, and the reasonable expectations of its stakeholders.

Hiring the Right People

Where the responsible criteria of the enterprise are clear, owners and managers can use people who exemplify the criteria to recruit and evaluate potential employees. By hiring people who embrace the responsible criteria of an enterprise, owners and managers take a large step toward having an effective business ethics program. It takes only one employee or agent to destroy the reputation of an enterprise. Hiring the wrong people increases the risk of criminal and civil liability and increases the costs of defending the enterprise or correcting any harm done. All of these risks adversely affect the prospects for improving business performance, making a profit, and increasing prosperity in the community.

To exercise due care, an enterprise must balance the reasonable expectations that applicants, employees, and agents have that an RBE will respect their privacy as individuals. Depending on the applicable employment protection laws, an RBE may screen prospective employees. Owners and managers should carefully research what screening processes an RBE may use in considering applications.

Owners and managers should also exercise due diligence in selecting their strategic alliances, the entities with which they merge, the entities they acquire, their joint venture partners, and their suppliers and service providers.

Placing People in the Right Positions

All enterprise positions are not the same as far as level of responsibility is concerned. Owners and managers must take care to ensure that their people are able to assume the level of responsibility that their positions demand.

Where high–level personnel are involved in misconduct, the enterprise itself is at greater risk. Government prosecutors, sentencing judges, the media, and the public, which might be inclined to treat an isolated incident of misconduct by lower–level personnel as an individual shortcoming, are more apt to attribute the misconduct of senior personnel to the enterprise as a whole.

Moreover, the conduct of managers and supervisors is a key indicator of the effectiveness of the business ethics program.

Outcomes are even more dramatic for supervisors: only 17 percent of employees observed misconduct where supervisors demonstrated all four ethics-related actions, but 35 percent observed misconduct where supervisors demonstrated fewer ethics-related actions, and 70 percent observed misconduct where supervisors only talked about ethics or took no action at all.

These associations between the ethics-related actions of managers and supervisors and expected program outcomes held true for the following outcomes as well: less feeling of pressure to compromise standards, more satisfaction with management's response to reported concerns, more sense that managers and supervisors are held accountable, and more satisfaction with the enterprise as a whole. Having the right people in the right places is essential for an enterprise to be a responsible business enterprise.

Retaining the Right People

Responsible people want to use their skills and knowledge in pursuit of a purpose they value. Compensation is important, but the sense of being a responsible member of a responsible enterprise has value in and of itself.

Having hired the right people, an RBE strives to assign them work they find worthwhile and challenging. It is *irresponsible* to assign a person who lacks the required capabilities to a responsible position.

Often the people most taken for granted are the good people who are trying to do the right thing and succeed. Owners and managers must be alert to practices that reward unscrupulous employees, while leaving conscientious employees feeling unrecognised and frustrated. Examples of this situation abound: sales commissions based on total sales that do not account for customer returns or complaints are but one.

Dealing with the Wrong People

From time to time, owners and managers make mistakes and hire or retain someone who does not share the reasonable criteria of the enterprise.

When owners and managers make mistakes in hiring, an RBE does neither these employees, their fellow employees, nor the enterprise any favour by having them remain in place. Where management's commitment is clear, employees and agents will often "self–select" themselves out of the enterprise. If they do not, owners and managers must take steps to remove them from the enterprise.

Often, the owner or senior manager is the "wrong person." This situation is a particular challenge for those who rely on SME goods or services, especially if the good or service requires the expertise of the owner. Large, complex enterprises (LCEs) may lose a critical part of their supply chains. More often, the best employees and agents seek employment elsewhere rather than have their livelihoods placed at risk, if they have the chance.

Sometimes other stakeholders, such as suppliers and even customers, may be the wrong people.

Encouraging Employees to Follow Standards and Procedures

Many management practices support responsible business conduct. These supportive management practices fall in three categories:

i) Recognising employee contributions

ii) Rewarding ethical behaviour

iii) Punishing unethical behaviour

Need for Recognition

The single most important thing that responsible owners and managers can do to encourage responsible business behaviour is to recognise the contributions their employees and agents make in pursuit of the purpose of the enterprise. Where managers have tasked employees with challenging work, they should recognise and commend successful completion.

Performance evaluations are an important means of recognising employee and agent behaviour. Core beliefs, standards and procedures, and reasonable stakeholder expectations should be important elements of the evaluation process. Managers and supervisors will also notice that they are not evaluated on whether they promote the responsible criteria among their subordinates.

i) Reward Systems

An important principle of management is that employees tend to do what is rewarded. If managers want responsible employee and agent behaviour that meets standards and procedures and that contributes to meeting reasonable stakeholder expectations, they should pay close attention to what they reward.

Commission schemes are the classic way that managers reward unethical behaviour and discourage ethical behaviour. If a value of the enterprise is customer service or excellence, the enterprise should aspire to customer satisfaction. However, sales agents and their managers are often compensated not by how well their customers are satisfied, but by how much product is sold. In one case, a sales agent, knowing that he was being transferred to another region, colluded with customers to order more products than were needed so that he would receive a bonus that the agent following him would otherwise have received. It is obvious that this "reward system" discourages ethical behaviour and encourages unethical behaviour.

Employees are quite skilled at finding out what is required for success in an enterprise. Although a code of conduct may say that customer service is a value, even one manager saying, "Do whatever it takes," dilutes the message. Sometimes the signal may be more subtle.

There is much opposition to rewarding ethical behaviour explicitly. First, there is a widespread sense that one should not reward people for doing what they should be doing anyway. Second, in organisational cultures that have a strong group orientation, rewards to an individual may be resented and may even make the individual uncomfortable. In such cultures, a reward to an individual may disrupt the harmony of the group.

The first point merits some further thought. As the sales bonus scheme above reflects, managers often reward people for doing what they should have done all along—in this case, selling products. What is the justification for such incentives? Perhaps to spur employees beyond what would otherwise be the minimum acceptable standard of performance.

If employees honestly fill out expense reports, as some authors suggest, the behaviour is so much the norm, that it makes no sense to reward it. However, consider the employee who reports an apparent violation of standards and procedures for the welfare of the enterprise when other employees do not. Although reporting concerns may be expected of all employees, it is not the norm in most enterprises. Substantial minorities of employees say they would never report misconduct they observed to managers.

Whatever the specific circumstances may be—and with due regard to the organisational culture—ethical behaviour that goes beyond the norms of conduct in the enterprise should be rewarded. Rewarding employees for reporting concerns makes a lot of sense if it is not the norm, and owners and managers should plan for it. The reward may also need to be made in private. The behaviour should certainly be reflected in performance evaluations.

Discipline Systems

Recognition and reward are two means of encouraging employees and agents to follow standards and procedures. But what should owners and managers do when standards and procedures are violated? They need to take all necessary steps to get the violator's attention and to prevent further violations, up to and including dismissal and reporting to law enforcement. They need to do this to protect the enterprise and its stakeholders from further harm.

Fairness is a concept that has a broader application. It is not fair to the enterprise or its stakeholders, including fellow employees, to fail to enforce standards and procedures. First, irresponsible behaviour does not help other employees meet the reasonable expectations of stakeholders. Second, a single act of misconduct may result in prosecution of the enterprise, civil claims, loss of reputation, and removal from preferred provider lists and strategic partnerships. Finally, if environment, health, and safety standards and procedures are violated, the welfare of other employees and the community is put at risk.

Allowing standards and procedures to be violated with impunity sends a powerful message. When managers fail to enforce their own standards, they signal that they do not believe in those standards.

Such questions arise particularly where employees perceive a double standard. Recent research suggests that employee perception of a business ethics program as primarily protecting owners and managers is the single most harmful factor to the prospects of the program's success.

One final consideration is to avoid the temptation to punish all employees for the violations of some of them by setting new standards or procedures. Often, if managers are uncomfortable with confronting an employee or agent about his or her behaviour, they instead admonish the group as a whole or establish another standard or procedure designed to encourage the desired behaviour.

Dealing with Mistakes, Misconduct, or Misunderstandings

Despite the best efforts of owners and managers, sometimes things go wrong. Even the most responsible business enterprises make mistakes. Standards and procedures will be violated, and reasonable stakeholder expectations will be dashed.

Owners and managers need to plan for mistakes, actual misconduct, and stakeholder misunderstanding of the enterprise's decisions and actions. At a minimum, they need to establish standards and procedures for dealing with such matters. Managers should be trained on how to exercise crisis management. They need to determine what steps to take to mitigate further harm or exposure: corrective action, restitution, voluntary disclosure, or any number of other remedial actions to compensate harmed stakeholders or prevent further violations.

Moreover, stakeholders that have been harmed by an enterprise's misconduct expect that they will be informed of a violation of standards that affects them, as well as that all harm done will be corrected, if possible.

Dealing Failures with and Mistakes

In many offices, one will find a sign that reads " To err is human, to forgive divine—neither of which is the policy of this company." However, an RBE recognizes that the employee who never fails is probably not contributing his or her fullest in pursuit of the enterprise's purpose. Much can be learned from failure, provided that the effort was intended to achieve enterprise ends and that the means were well chosen and within enterprise boundaries.

An RBE fosters an environment in which the creativity and enthusiasm of its employees and agents are encouraged even in the face of mistakes and failure. There is no surer way of preventing creativity than to punish employees for mistakes made in good faith.

It reinforces the responsibility that employees and agents assumc: to make rcsponsible choices and to take responsible actions to achieve the ends of the enterprise. It is also a liberating policy, which tends to free employees and agents from the fear of unfair criticism or punishment if they make mistakes or fail.

A responsible response to mistakes of employees includes an evaluation of what happened, and why. It includes a sincere effort to learn from mistakes or failure. Managers may need to modify the standards and procedures that failed to prevent the misconduct.

Dealing with Misconduct or Serious Harm to Stakeholders

It is important to distinguish mistakes from misconduct. Misconduct is intentional, negligent, or reckless disregard for the core beliefs, established standards and procedures, and reasonable expectations of the stakeholders of the enterprise.

For example, it is no excuse that a choice or action, such as bribing a government official to make a sale, might contribute to achieving the financial ends of the enterprise in the short run. First, it is not clear that making sales through bribery ever contributes to the welfare of an enterprise in either the short or the long run. Second, owners and managers set the standard precisely because they decided that bribery raises an unacceptable risk to the enterprise.

Owners and managers respond to misconduct in the same way they respond to a mistake—by evaluating what happened and why.

When the misconduct is a violation of law or a stakeholder is seriously harmed, a number of other steps must be considered.

i) Voluntary Disclosure

When an employee or agent violates the law on behalf of the enterprise, both thc individual and the enterprise may be open to prosecution. As a matter of responsible policy, owners and managers must consult with local counsel regarding the advisability of voluntary disclosure to the government.

First, employees need to know what the policy is and how seriously owners and managers take their admonition to obey the law. Second, in many jurisdictions, voluntary disclosure will be treated as good corporate citizenship, and punishment may be limited to the individual alone.

Finally, the risk of prosecution and harsh penalties against the enterprise often increases dramatically if the government discovers the violation and learns that the enterprise concealed it.

As two authors note, there are a number of potential dangers in failing to voluntarily disclose a violation: if the government discovers a violation, damage to the credibility of the enterprise may be irreparable. Government agencies are more likely to prosecute if the government discovers a violation. The failure to disclose is more likely to be seen as a cover-up, perhaps to protect senior management. If a subsequent violation occurs, the failure to disclose may be used against the enterprise at the later trial.

Where the rule of law is not the norm, owners and managers must carefully examine the relevant context of the enterprise in establishing its policy and seek professional advice. Nevertheless, owners and managers must also consider the organisational culture and the effect that failing to take responsibility for misconduct will have on the attitudes of employees.

Where extortion by agency officials can be expected when an RBE reports its' misconduct, it is important that an RBE not deal with this situation in isolation. If extortion is expected, owners and managers should plan to work with trade associations and non-governmental organisations (NGOs) to reduce their exposure. Since a primary tool in the fight against corruption is transparency, trade associations and NGOs can support enterprises that voluntarily disclose their misconduct by issuing their public statements targeting the offending agency or by otherwise bringing pressure to bear on the agency to reduce extortion.

In any event, responsible managers must establish a policy to govern how they will deal with misconduct before it happens, when their judgment is clearest. In this way, they can identify gaps in capability.

Cooperation with the Government

Accepting responsibility and voluntarily disclosing misconduct to the government may be followed by a government inquiry or investigation. Or the government may make unannounced visits to the enterprise.

How the enterprise responds to government requests has potentially serious legal implications. Responsible managers will establish a policy that governs how the enterprise will respond to government requests. Such a policy supports employees and agents in making the responsible decision to cooperate.

The standards and procedures should be developed with legal counsel familiar with the laws and practices of the jurisdictions in which the enterprise does business. Whom they should contact for advice, including legal counsel, should be clear as well. Having such policies and procedures helps ensure that employees act responsibly and avoid mistakes that may be costly to the enterprise.

i) Corrective Action

As a general principle, an RBE takes all appropriate steps to cure any harm it has caused stakeholders. These steps include compensating victims, stopping operations, recalling products, restoring the environment to its previous condition, and taking steps to prevent future harm.

Where further harm can be predicted, such as health problems that can take decades to manifest themselves, an RBE may set up a trust fund for stakeholders damaged by its misconduct.

Handling Misunderstandings and Other Crises

Sometimes a crisis is not of the enterprise's making. What does an RBE do when accused of shortcomings it did not commit? Responsible management works through such misunderstandings. The general principle is to learn how to pursue the enterprise's purpose and meet reasonable stakeholder expectations by engaging stakeholders when appropriate.

During an intense period of information gathering and deliberation, two independent management teams considered as many as 150 alternatives for dealing with the crisis. Eventually, it recovered and even increased its market share. Although the experts were predicting that Tylenol, as a brand, would not last a year, "What those experts failed to anticipate was the public reaction to what was perceived as a deliberate act of corporate responsibility that was beautifully executed and skillfully followed up with a well–designed recovery plan."

The decision to recall Tylenol was based on the Johnson & Johnson "Credo," first drafted in 1943. Although the decision was made by the chief executive officer, it reflected the organisational culture of the enterprise as a whole.

Modifying the Business Ethics Program

Finally, where mistakes, misconduct, and misunderstandings occur, the responsible business constantly evaluates its performance. It uses such incidents as opportunities to learn how the business ethics program is performing. The essential question is, "Does this enterprise have an effective business ethics program?"

Responsible management practices are critical to the success of an RBE in improving its business performance, increasing the prosperity of its community, and contributing to the social capital in its markets by learning to meet the reasonable expectations of its shareholders. Owners and managers of an RBE develop responsible management practices by answering these three questions:

i) How can we ensure that we have the right people in the right places while we pursue our purpose as an enterprise?

ii) How can we encourage our employees and agents to follow our standards and procedures?

iii) What do we owe our stakeholders when mistakes, misconduct, or misunderstandings occur that involve our established standards and procedures or their reasonable expectations?

To have the right people in the right places in the enterprise involves using the enterprise's core beliefs, standards and procedures, and reasonable stakeholder expectations to establish responsible criteria.

To encourage employees and agents to follow enterprise standards and procedures, pursue the enterprise's purpose, and meet reasonable stakeholder expectations, responsible managers evaluate decisions and activities according to the responsible criteria, and they reward and discipline employees and agents as appropriate.

When things go wrong for an RBE, responsible managers address mistakes, misconduct, and misunderstandings.They learn from mistakes and failures made in good faith.

REFERENCES

Allison, R. (2005). *The Birth of Spiritual Economics Spirituality and ethics in management*. L. Zsolnai. New York, Springer. 19: 61–74.

Anand, V. and C. C. Rosen (2008). "The Ethics of Organizational Secrets". *Journal of Management Inquiry* 17(2). 97–101.

Borgerson, J. L. and J. E. Schroeder (2008). *Building an Ethics of Visual Representation: Contesting Epistemic Closure in Marketing Communication. Cutting Edge Issues in Business Ethics*. M. P. Morland and P. Werhane. Boston, Springer: 87–108.

Boxall, P. and J. Purcell (2007). *Strategic management and human resources: the pursuit of productivity, exibility, and legitimacy. Human Resource Management: Ethics and Employment*. A. H. Pinnington, R. Macklin and T. Campbell. Oxford, Oxford University Press: 66–80.

10

Managing the Risks of Business Ethics

The risks of an ethical misconduct disaster have never been greater due to the complexity of the global business environment. Increasing regulation and enforcement as well as stakeholder scrutiny can create an unexpected organisational crisis.

One approach to understanding business ethics is to take an individual perspective and focus on personal morals, character and the person. This approach assumes that virtues linked to the high moral ground of truthfulness, honesty, and fairness are self-evident and easy to apply in a complex global environment. This approach would assume that organisational values and ethics training may be more appropriate for individuals with unacceptable moral development. Another approach to understanding business ethics is to assume that organisational values and compliance systems are necessary to prevent people from engaging in unethical conduct. This approach recognizes the risks and the complex decision-making environment in a global environment. Business ethics programs and organisations combine values and compliance, which requires training and constant vigilance.

The scandals and unethical conduct that have occurred globally have taught us that some people deliberately break the law or engage in inappropriate behaviour. Many others never see ethical issues when devising what they think as an innovative scheme for success. In the U.S. the Supreme Court and the Federal Sentencing Guidelines for Organisations (FSGO) hold organisations responsible for the conduct of their employees, most firms have decided to implement ethics and compliance programs to prevent misconduct and diminish the risk associated with employee wrongdoing. The 2004 Amendments to the FSGO hold the governing authority, usually the board of directors, responsible for ethical leadership including an effective ethics program and internal ethics audits. Even though the majority of employees want to do the right thing, many people don't know the exact nature of the law and are totally surprised when they are charged with violations that were never anticipated. The legal system and the nature of civil litigation make ethical decision making a 'mine field' for possible error without adequate knowledge of the potential risk of a decision.

Managers need to understand how ethical decisions are made and the environment that influences ethical decision making. Managers face the same business ethics risks as others but managers should be more aware of those special risks associated with customer contact and interaction with their relevant stakeholders.

Many managers have a difficult time understanding that ethics requires going beyond minimal legal requirements. Trying to find a framework that helps managers see the benefits of conducting oneself according to the highest ethical standards is difficult indeed.

The Ethics Resource Center reported, in the 2005 National Business Ethics Survey (NBES), that 52% of employees observed at least one type of misconduct in the past year. Just over half (55%) reported the misconduct to management, a 10 percentage point decrease since the 2003 NBES survey.

The reality is that employees are at a high risk for observing or engaging in misconduct. According to the NBES survey, in the last year one-third of all employees encountered a situation at work that they think invites ethical misconduct. Formal programs and strong ethical cultures significantly reduce the pressure to engage in misconduct, the observation of misconduct, and the need to report misconduct. In fact, no firm with a strong ethics program for 10 years has had a major ethical scandal in the last 5 years. The U.S. Sentencing Commission reports that no firms with an effective ethics program have had significant legal or reputation damage in the last 5 years.

Stakeholders Define Marketing Ethics Issues

A stakeholder perspective facilitates the understanding of how agreements, collaborations, and even confrontations exist on ethics issues. Stakeholders designate the individuals or groups that can directly or indirectly affect, or be affected by, a firm's activities. Stakeholders can be viewed as both internal and external. Internal stakeholders include functional departments, employees, boards of directors, and managers.

Another view of stakeholders characterizes them as primary or secondary. Primary stakeholders are those whose continued participation is absolutely necessary for business survival; they consist of employees, customers, investors, suppliers, and shareholders that provide necessary infrastructure. Secondary stakeholders are not usually engaged in transactions with the business and are not essential for its survival; they include the media, trade associations, non-governmental organisations, along with other interest groups. Unhappy customers may be viewed with less urgency than negative press stories that can damage a business. Highly visible secondary stakeholders such as an interest group or the media may at times be viewed with greater concern than employees or customers. The three critical elements in assessing stakeholder influence are their power, legitimacy and urgency of issues.

Power has been defined as "the ability to exercise ones will over others". Legitimacy relates to socially accepted and expected structures that help define whose concerns or claims really count and urgency captùres the dynamics of the time-sensitive nature of stakeholder interactions.

Shared Ethical Values and Norms

Major stakeholders may have different needs and a fine-grained approach may be needed to ascertain even differences within major stakeholder groups, such as customers, employees, suppliers, and investors. On the other hand, usually, a certain number of individual stakeholders share similar ethical values and norms.

Stakeholder Issues in Business

Stakeholder ethical values and norms apply to a variety of business issues such as sales practices, consumer rights, environmental protection, product safety, and proper information disclosure. Noticeably, stakeholder values and norms concern both issues that do and do not affect stakeholders' own welfare. Stakeholder issues are the concerns that stakeholders embrace about organisational activities and the residual impact.

A Framework for Understanding Organisational Ethical Decision Making

In understanding marketing ethics it is necessary to understand how people make ethical decisions. Within the context of an organisation, there is an ethical component to business decisions and this decision maybe influenced by the organisation, the specific situation, or pressure exerted by co–workers. External stakeholder interests, concerns or dilemmas help trigger ethical issue intensity. Organisational culture and individual moral philosophies and values influence the recognition of ethical issues and business ethics decisions. The decisions or outcomes are evaluated by both internal and external stakeholders.

First, as previously discussed, organisations can identify the importance of stakeholders and stakeholder issues, and gather information to respond to significant individuals, groups, and communities. Next, in the decision-making process, managers should identify the importance or relevance of a perceived issue. The intensity of a particular issue is likely to vary over time and among individuals and is influenced by the organisational culture, values and norms; the special characteristics of the situation; and the personal pressures weighing on the decision. Personal moral development and philosophy, organisational culture, and coworkers, determine why different people perceive issues with varying intensity.

Perhaps one of the greatest challenges facing the study of business ethics involves the role of individuals and their values. However, individual factors are obviously important in the evaluation and resolution of ethical issues, and familiarity with theoretical frameworks from the field of moral philosophy is helpful in determining ethical decision making in business. Two significant factors in organisational ethics are an individual's personal moral philosophy and stage of moral development. This socialisation occurs from family, friends, formal education, religion, and other philosophical frameworks that an individual may embrace.

Although individuals must make ethical choices, it is also true that they often make these decisions in committees, group meetings, and through discussion with colleagues. Ethical decisions in the workplace are guided by the organisation's culture and the influence of others, such as coworkers, superiors, subordinates.

The ethical climate of an organisation is a significant element of organisational culture. Whereas a firm's overall culture establishes ideals that guide a wide range of behaviours for members of the organisation, its ethical climate focuses specifically on issues of right and wrong. Codes of conduct and ethics policies, top management's actions on ethical issues, the values and moral development and philosophies of coworkers, and the opportunity for misconduct all contribute to an organisation's ethical climate.

Organisations can manage their culture and ethical climate by trying to hire employees whose values match their own. Some firms even measure potential employees' values during the hiring process and strive to choose individuals who "fit" within the ethical climate rather than those whose beliefs and values differ significantly. A poor "fit" can have very expensive ramifications for both organisations and employees.

Together, organisational culture and the influence of coworkers may foster conditions that limit or permit misconduct. When these conditions provide rewards, such as financial gain, recognition, promotion, or simply the good feeling from a job well done – the opportunity for unethical conduct may be encouraged, or discouraged, based on ethical climate. Organisational policies, processes, and other factors may contribute to the opportunity to act unethically.

Opportunity usually relates to employees' immediate job context– where they work, with whom they work, and the nature of the work. The specific work situation includes the motivational "carrots and sticks" that superiors can use to influence employee behaviour. Pay raises, bonuses, and public recognition are carrots, or positive reinforcement, whereas reprimands, pay penalties, demotions, and even firings act as sticks, the negative reinforcement. This framework helps managers put ethical decision making in organisational context and see how the process fits together. Once one begins to understand that good ethics is linked to organisational performance they see why it is necessary to have organisational ethics and compliance programs. Also, managers begin to see the personal costs including reputation damage from misconduct.

From Ethical Misconduct Disasters: Enron and Daewoo

Enron

The Enron disaster and trial provides an excellent case to examine organisational ethical decision making. It underscores how complex ethical decisions are in a large corporation. On May 25th 2006 a Houston jury found Enron CEO's Ken Lay and Jeff Skilling guilty on all counts of conspiring to hide the company's financial condition in 2000 and 2001. During the case the judge dealt a blow to the two defendants when he told the jury that they could find the defendants guilty of consciously avoiding knowing about wrongdoing at the company. Many former Enron employees refused to testify because they were not guaranteed that their testimony would not be used against them at future trials convicting them. The verdict was a total victory for federal prosecutors who had spent four years building a criminal case against the two men who had played a key role in building Enron as a role model for the energy industry. The verdict was a blow to Lay and Skilling who testified that 'Enron was a fundamentally sound company brought low in a market panic spurred by short sellers and negative media reports.'

The jury found Lay, 64, guilty of six counts of conspiracy and fraud, Skilling, 52, was convicted on 18 counts of conspiracy and securities fraud but acquitted on nine out of 10 counts of illegal insider trading. On the way out of the courtroom Lay said he was "shocked" by the verdict. "I firmly believe I am innocent of the charges against me as I've said from day one." Then juror Wendy Vaughan said "I felt it was their duty to know what was going on."

While many people can't work up much sympathy for Mr. Skilling and Mr. Lay because so many people lost a lot of money, there is an alternative viewpoint. A number of law professors and lawyers have concerns about the Enron Task Force's prosecution of Ken Lay and Jeff Skilling, accusing the government of "criminalising corporate agency costs." In other words the government is accused of misusing criminal laws to punish questionable business transactions and bad management decisions. There is no doubt that this was a very complex case and even the most hard core antibusiness types are queasy with the conclusion of this tragedy. There was not conclusive evidence that there was intent to defraud investors, although investor losses were massive.

The truth of the matter is that the jury would have had to understand the entire corporate culture as well as many systemic embedded business decisions at Enron to know for sure that Lay and Skilling were guilty of their charges. Bad business decisions were made but there is uncertainty as to the true involvement and intent of many of the CEO's decisions. Society and the courts tend to simplify events and blame all that goes wrong on just a few individuals. In thesociety we are taught that the opinion of trusted professionals such as accountants and lawyers can be followed in business decisions. In this case the accounting firm Arthur Andersen, internal and external attorneys, as well as the board of directors approved the key decisions at Enron.

Mr. Lay said he never intended to harm any one, in fact, he came back as CEO after Jeff Skilling stepped down and at the insistence of the Enron board of directors to providc lcadcrship and attempt to save the company. A decision now, that he and his wife both regret. As CEO, Lay was responsible for 30,000 employees operating in 30 countries. He managed an exceptional group of employees, as eluded to in the film *Enron: The Smartest Men in the Room.* Great leaders are often given accolades for their accomplishments and Lay was no exception in the 'hey day' of Enron.

Daewoo

Kim Woo Choong, founder of the defunct Daewoo Group, was convicted of fraud and embezzlement, sentenced to 10 years in prison and ordered to forfeit more than $22 billion, after his leadership role in the biggest business failure in South Korean history. The trial was watched closely in South Korea and the world and was considered by many as a test of whether the justice system extended to the leaders of a major business.

Mr. Kim, 69 years old, started Daewoo as a small textile-trading firm in 1967, building it into a conglomerate of more than 30 companies by the 1990s, with products as diverse as cars, ships and televisions. But his zeal for growth, fuelled by debt-funded acquisitions, helped drive the group into bankruptcy in 1999, two years after the Asian financial crisis exposed Daewoo's weaknesses. Could it have been prevented through ethical leadership and corporate culture that focused on global ethical and legal risks?

South Korean banks and the government incurred billions of dollars in losses in the collapse. Mr. Kim fled the country soon after the collapse, staying mainly in France. During his exile, workers in former Daewoo factories pasted up "Wanted" posters depicting Mr. Kim. When he returned to the country from Vietnam, he emerged from the airport to a crowd of protesters and a bank of bright lights and TV cameras.

Mr. Kim's defense lawyers argued that one person alone didn't cause Daewoo to collapse and cited a variety of other reasons, including the cash crunch it wound up in by investing in overseas currencies as a hedge against the then-falling won. Similar to Enron, a culture of pushing the envelope and a great deal of complacency on the part of employees and stakeholders created the disaster. Both the Daewoo Group and Enron required more than one person to damage the company. It required a corporate culture of cooperation and complacency involving many employees and many failures by multiple stakeholders.

References

Dembinski, P. H., C. Lager, et al., Eds. (2006). *Enron and World Finance: A Case Study in Ethics*. New York, Palgrave.

Jones, C., M. Parker, et al. (2005). *For Business Ethics: A Critical Text*. London, Routledge.

11

Corporate Social Responsibility

Nowadays, the argument concerned about the triple bottom line is very hot in the studies of Corporate Social responsibility (CSR) and socially responsible investment (SRI). It is assumed that TBL legitimates CSR activities and SRI. CSR intend to do social and environmental activities and SRI finances CSR activities. In these arguments, the perspective of CSR seems to be a lack of economical perspective and thought that, but actually the economical perspective is set up as a basic line in CSR. In general, CSR activities are misunderstood, so CSR activities are regarded as just social oriented activities. This misunderstanding is caused by emphasising on gaining profits and its maximisation as CSR in neo-classical context.

CSR activities is not new, they have already more than 100 years history. Originally CSR came from charity principle or nobles oblige. This means some firms or some rich people, that afford to help community or others because of their profits or richness, did CSR activities by which firms and rich people do not earn the money, but only spend money. But nowadays CSR is not so, doing CSR activities enable us to earn the money. This is proved through existence of SRI market. SRI market extends so rapidly and so many people invest SRI funds. Investments of SRI funds mean that not only people support CSR activities of firms, but also they could expect return. TBL includes not only social, environmental perspectives, but also economical perspective. TBL also supports and strengthens CSR activities in theoretical aspect.

SRI makes also new perspective. SRI market developing and expanding shows us that how important to gain profit is, even if firms are engaged in social activities. We regard the expansion of SRI market and some above normal successful firms in SRI market as evidences that social activities are accepted and firms could gain profits.

In real business, we can see that a firm is engaged in doing business connected with a sense of TBL and succeed with its activity. TBL has been applied to strategic management.

Before we see SRI and CSR activities, we would like to think of CSR. As above described, CSR is not new. In 1950s in U.S, social problems like environmental pollution which caused by firms occurred and were accused by citizen were discussed as corporate social responsibility. In 1960s and 70s CSR was very hot issue in USA again, because some illegal action ware accused and some big incidents occurred in business and politics. So many people paid attention to firms' activities which could cause them harm. In other words, firms' influence was huge and people could not ignore it. To survive, keep developing and justify its existence, firms were in the situation to persuade people and care of them. Then social issues were begun to discuss in CSR. CSR is regarded as social issue in management in this context.

When thinking of CSR, we need to think of stakeholder theory. Stakeholder theory takes existence who a firm affects and by whom firm is affected into account. In stakeholder theory context, a firm is assumed that a firm is a social existence, even though a firm accepts or do not accept it. A firm takes stakeholder into account, when a firm acts. Of course, a firm keeps having an economic interest. This attitude is described as "socially aware without giving up their (firms) economic self-interest". An activity of a firm is based on stakeholders. On the contrary, stakeholders give a firm pressure to act socially oriented. These engagements are sometimes so strong and a firm could not ignore, because stakeholder have a power against a firm. Source of this power is connected with dependency. On one side, a firm could not exist without stakeholders, on another side stakeholders could not exist without a firm. This dependency is based on each resource. There are implicit and explicit contracts among stakeholders and a firm. This justifies power of stakeholders. To extent this, potential stakeholders have also a power, because it is possible to have a contact a firm in future, to be a customer, etc.

Nowadays we could not discuss CSR without stakeholder theory, because a firm's purpose is not only to survive, develop and justify its existence, but also to do business with stakeholders, to develop society, to support society, to solve social problems and to gain sustainability. CSR concepts are still spreading.

Function of Socially Responsible Investment (SRI)

SRI utilizes the mechanism of a market. And the company which is socially responsible is evaluated. Self-initiative and morality of company and law are not entrusted. An individual and an institutional investor will give the sanction of plus or minus to the company information which the evaluation organisation which is performing the social screen. There are three forms in SRI.

Social Screening

Social screening is determining investment not only including a financial index but consideration of as opposed to society or environment for a company. There are positive screen and negative screen in social screening.

Positive screen is to industry with much social criticism which makes an investment.

Negative screen is to industry with much social criticism which does not make an investment.

Shareholder Activism

It is positively concerned with a firm from a stockholder's position. And it is affecting management and a plan. It aims at the improvement issue through a dialogue with a firm. And it is the purpose to boost going concern value.

Social Investment

i) *Community Development Investment:* This is investment

performed for the purpose of economical development support of the declined area.

ii) *Socially Development Investment:* This is the loan and investment to the entity which undertakes social works, such as natural energy.

iii) *Socially Responsible Government Expenditure:* This is considering the influence which it has on the public investment, in case the government's makes public investment.

SRI affects business management through the power of investment as mentioned above. It evaluates positively the firm which is socially responsible, and does not evaluate the firm which has not done responsibility. The low firm of social and environmental achievements is no longer evaluated from a market. Because it is shown that a potential risk is high. It will become impossible for such a firm to already survive.

Recently Transition of SRI Market

United States

According to investigation of Good Money, 100 billion-dollar scale and the SRI market were presumed in 1985. It exceeded 400 billion dollars in 89, and expanded by 6 times in 600 billion dollars and six years in 1991. The growth rate of the first half of the 90s stagnates. Investigation of Social Investment Forum (SIF) shows the SRI market remained in 639 billion dollars in 95 and afterwards. The scandal of Enron or WorldCom became a cause from 2001 to 2002, and the concern about the state of corporate governance, the crisis management system of a firm, and the measure of CSR increased further.

Europe

A spread of SRI in Europe has got into stride quickly after the 1990s. Britain of the SRI market in Europe is 224,500 million pound. The price of the SRI market of other European countries is 198 euros to it. Britain will look at also in Europe mainly by Britain which is the SRI market of the maximum scale. According to investigation of Ethical

Investment Research Service (EIRIS) about a SRI investment fund, it will be about 200 million pound in 1989. However, it has accomplished about 4 billion pound and 20 times as many growths as this in 2001.

Japan

It is the beginning of full-scale SRI in 1999. And many SRI funds appeared in 1999. It began from the "Ecofund" of Nikko asset management, and the "ASUNOHANE" of the Asahi life asset management which set the evaluation axis as the social side was put on the market. When transition of the asset balance of the general invitation investment fund market of SRI was seen, it exceeded 200 billion yen in 1999. Then, that a stock price falls in reaction followed and it decreased even to 60 billion yen in 2003. However, the concern about SRI is becoming still higher. The time when the firm which makes environment and a social achievement also in Japan is evaluated will come.

Sociality and Environmental Consciousness are Purpose of Firm or only Instrument of Firm to Gain Profit?

The expansion of SRI market means that CSR activities including sociality, environmental consciousness and economical are accepted in thesociety, but it is also possible to think that some firms use these thinking as strategic instruments. It is not so problematic, but a problem is that stakeholders are regarded as instruments to gain profit or use stakeholders as instruments. In other words, economical perspective is a higher rank perspective than Sociality and environmental consciousness, which are only the instruments for gaining it. Originally Freeman has described that firm treats stakeholders equally and as ends rather than mere means according to neo-Kantian principle. To emphasise on profit maximisation is based on how firm divides its profit for shareholders. A firm only does duty to a shareholder. This discussion on using sociality and environmental consciousness to gain profit is assumed that there is principal and agency problem. This relationship can be drawn that shareholder as capital provider and firm as managing by using this capital. So firm do business to make money for its principal. This relationship is different from relationship between shareholder and firm in SRI market, it is only financial relationship. So firm has take only financial aspect into account, so concentrates on only profit. Shareholders are just only one of stakeholders, they don't have special advantage. As Miyasaka has suggested, in stakeholder theory, principal-agency relationship in stakeholder theory context can be supposed in non-financial relationship, including not only shareholder but also another stakeholders, because a relation with other stakeholders could be thought as important more than at a relation with a shareholders in firms' activities. As above described, a firm is dependent not only on shareholders, but also on stakeholders concerned about resources. Then, the concept of sociality and environment consciousness comes out. A firm is expected by the stakeholder as existence which realizes their purposes not only economical but socially and environmental. And/or it is expected that a firm activities don't influence negative effect on stakeholders. Therefore it is assumed that there is non-financial principal-agency relationship among stakeholder. A firm takes responsible for requirement of stakeholders. However, many stakeholders who were the non-financial principal-agency relationship as it saw in SRI markets actually become a stockholder, and take part in firm management increasingly. Until now, it has been seen that there was non- financial relationship between firm and stakeholders except for shareholders, so firms have not had explicit responsibilities for stakeholders. It was dependent on firm's own will to have responsibilities for stakeholder. But in context of SRI, this investment means that investors invest firm's activities, namely CSR activities and/or its sense of value, sociality, environmental consciousness and a stakeholder accepts that the consciousness that the company has responsibility in the stakeholders and supports it. Furthermore, such an activity shows potentially a possibility that each stakeholder will become a shareholder. At the same time a firm should keep having the consciousness that a firm have responsibilities in stakeholders who are not shareholders.

Environmental

As seen above, sociality and environmental consciousness are important to do business in context of CSR, of course economical perspective, too. These three sets of perspectives are components of TBL. On the one hand historically, product development, production, marketing, human resource has been developed in many firms in economical perspective, so core competence of a firm is closely concerned with pursuit of profit. On the other side, sociality and environmental consciousness are relatively new issues in doing business. These were not cores in business, but just support or assist core competence. Toyota Prius is good example. Toyota Prius are sold very well and still now. This success is very important to think CSR activities, because this success factors are not only its fuel-efficient engine, not also this car stimulates the customer who has interested in environmental and/or has environmental consciousness. It is supported by many people and is still continuing selling. We can see this phenomenon as a proof that many people are conscious of environmental consciousness.

Furthermore, extent of environmental consciousness is pointed out also in that the companies which gain ISO have been increasing in number steadily. If the firms which gained ISO increase in number, the meaning as a standard of ISO will become thin. But this functions as a bottom line or entry barrier. In other words, the firm which has not gained has to gain ISO or other standards which are set sometimes by firm itself and explains stakeholders them to entry market. And it is expected that the firms keep tackling environmental problems and solve them. But only responding to stakeholders' requirement is not connected with core competence of firm. It does not lead to competitive advantage. Although it does not lead competitive advantage of a firm, since it was set up as the bottom line, a firm has to follow it.

Sociality

When considering the sociality, fairness in competition becomes important. "Can a firm do anything, in order to gain profits?" This question always is mentioned concerned about sociality, CSR and business ethics. Here is assumed that a firm does anything not to break a rule in context of profit maximisation, but not to break a rule is not sociality, not ethical and not corresponding to CSR. It is not fairness. It is not necessary to mention it by us. But sometimes these conducts do not work well, but there is no meaning. Some cases show us that, World com, Enron, etc. Setting up own rule and at the same time doing business following own rules could lead to competitive advantage, but it is only possible, not certain.

Body shop is good example in this context. Body shop contracts suppliers who protect rules which are very severe and pay reasonable price for productions. Price standards are not set up by standards of product country, but by Body shop. Normally prices are higher than in other transactions, but these activities make customers trust Body shop and customers support these activities. This strategy that Body shop sets up own rule and does business following own rules is connected with core competence of Body shop and leads to competitive advantage. Though Body shop is not so big, but its presence is certain.

Role of Bottom Line

Before we see how a firm manages CSR, we think of a meaning of an appearance of such a firm like Toyota. It has a big meaning, because such a firm plays a role as bottom line. For example, Toyota is a big landmark in auto industry, which succeeded in introducing a new style of car and finding eco market. If the other firm in auto industry regard Toyota as first mover, this is also a big meaning, because some firms try to entry this market, and in order to entry this market they have to develop own techniques based on environmental consciousness. Toyota's standards play a role as an entry barrier in eco market or in future general car market.

On the other side, Body shop success is also one big step. Body shop is not so big in comparison with Toyota. Its activity is in so called niche market. Having sociality and environmental consciousness is accepted in such a small market, leads to competitive advantage and is connected with core competence. To a contrary, appearance of such a firm urges SRI market to expand. Anyway, sociality and environmental consciousness are caught as it is a request from stakeholders.

A firm striving to realise sociality and environmental consciousness in business fields actually sets up market bottom lines. The idea of TBL helps these movements, but TBL in itself does not set up market bottom line.

CSR MANAGEMENT

As seen above, it can guess that a SRI market develops. It is necessary for Japanese firms to build the management system by which it is evaluated in a SRI market. CSR is asked in product development, production, marketing, human resource, investor relations, and all the management processes of philanthropy.

In such a flow, many of Japanese firms strengthened the measure for CSR activity in response to the trend of a European and American firm, or the guideline's in 2003. Also in Sony and UniCharm, establishment of a CSR organisation continued the CSR room of Ricoh in January, 2003 taking advantage of installation. The movement toward organisation maintenance is also made continuously now, and examination of the organisation of a CSR room or a CSR committee is progressing. Moreover, use for social improvement with the application of compliance about specific goods at trading conditions. Practice of desirable CSR is raising competitiveness and firm value continuously, when a firm does social responsibility. In order to realise this, based on business environment, it is necessary to discern what serves as the fountainhead of competitiveness. And the vision and strategy of CSR need to unify and it is necessary to function.

Establishment of CSR Vision

It is necessary to decide upon the CSR vision based on the uniqueness and environment of a firm. That is because a concrete measure is not clearly performed even if it builds the structure of CSR. Moreover, it responds to the enterprise characteristic which the firm is developing, or the business environment placed. It becomes the process which finds out the original theme which complements a weak point by it taking advantage of a strong point.

The Basic Commitment of the Toshiba Group and the Group slogan,"Committed to People, Committed to the Future. Toshiba.", is the concrete expression of both therelationships with stakeholders and thebusiness activities. The first step of CSR activity was discriminating the role in the society of Toshiba from electronics in the light of the participation to energy.

By the technical innovation in these fields, it is doing its best in the Toshiba group in order to complete the mission.

Stakeholder Relations

In order to build a CSR strategy based on change of a stakeholders' action, it is necessary to grasp periodically the consciousness of a stockholder, a customer, an employee, and a customer, and change of a sense of values. For that purpose, a dialogue with a stakeholder is an effective means. This is it not only hearing the opinion of a stakeholder, but making use of in management. It is raising reliance through communication with a customer, a stockholder, an employee, and a community.

Plan–Do–Check–Action Management

In order to connect CSR to continuous development, it is necessary to take in an element to business at CSR. It cannot demonstrate an effect, if it cannot be reflected in management even if it recognizes the vision of CSR, and a demand of a stakeholder. It is required for practice of CSR to build the structure of PDCA.

Establishment of CSR Department

The business for achieving CSR is construction of a management system. The whole organisation design also about CSR is called for like the existing management system. As making an organisation, installation of the officer specialising in CSR is indispensable. It builds the CSR committee which crosses a function and its post for this officer at the top. There are also many places which take charge of CSR as extension of activity of an environmental department or a philanthropy department at present. CSR is positioned as corporate strategy.

In Toshiba, it recognizes the importance of CSR anew against the background of progress of enterprise globalisation, and a rise of the request from society. It positions CSR into corporate management and is advancing systematically. And it established CSR headquarters newly as an organisation president under the direct control in July, 2003, and fixed whole company promotion organisation. It held the

CSR promotion committee which it constitutes from officers including the CSR division manager. It has decided the direction of the activity by the statement of principles and important matter of whole company CSR activity into the whole group.

Reporting System

CSR management starts in the vision and organisation design which tackle CSR. It builds organisation based on this direction, and develops activity. By building the organisation of CSR, leading to improvement in performance is important. It sets up the target of the performance as an organisation. And it carries out the monitoring of whether it is performed. It is necessary to report as an index which shows the result of activity to a stakeholder. It is important to perform corporate activity which is responsible to society, and to achieve accountability to a stakeholder.

MANAGING CSR ACTIVITIES

As above described, it is very important for a firm to think CSR and manage CSR activities. But it is not easy to carry out because of a lack of financial resource, human resources who have qualification of environmental studies, or other resource. A big firm can afford to pay these, for example hire human resource or educate employees. But other firms sometimes cannot carry out, but they have to do it because it is requirement of their stakeholders. As above seen, nowadays a firm is expected that a firms does business with having sense of TBL, some firms have already showed these model and strengthen their presence. If their presence is much stronger, it is difficult for a firm who acts without sense of TBL to gain profit or to survive. In some markets, a part of TBL has been already regarded as standards like quality control managements (QCM), especially environmental oriented activity. And it is also difficult for a firm to gain competitive advantage by only introducing TBL.

Does SRI market really encourage a firm to do CSR activities? It is also problematic, because some empirical studies have already examined that correlation positively or negatively between CSR activities and SRI are almost not observed. But we have to consider why SRI market has expanded within these 15 years. We think that it is one of the factors which encourage a firm to do CSR activities. And we can also think of effect of screening of SRI funds, when we think of correlation between SRI and CSR activities. SRI funds make a decision according to consequences of screening. Some firms are regarded as worth to invest and the other are regarded as not worth to invest. It is possible for a firm which is engaged in CSR activities to be excluded by SRI funds in this process. What does it mean for this firm? According to evaluation a firm can improve its activities and could do better than before. It stimulates also the other firms to improve their action and could produce good social outcome as a whole.

A lack of evaluation system of SRI funds is also problematic. Schepers and Sethi indicated in their paper that there are so many differences among SRI funds, for example, criteria of screening, methods of screening and purpose of SRI funds. They have examined four issues concerned about this,

i) Definitional problem,

ii) Inconsistent screening,

iii) Selection criteria and

iv) CSR attributes.

So we think that it is very important to evaluate and compare SRI funds. It is possible that some SRI funds which are regarded as SRI funds are actually not SRI funds. In this context, we have to judge more carefully the expansion of SRI market and its meaning.

Do sociality and environmental consciousness really lead to competitive advantage? It is also difficult to answer. As we have suggested, Toyota has showed us that product which is designed by environmental perspective succeeded and found a new market in Japan. And this led to competitive advantage. Environmental consciousness has been internalised already in routine works so long time. Toyota's achievement is that Toyota has enhanced the value of these minds up to strategic level. This is not easy, but to keep having sociality and environmental consciousness could enable a firm to get competitive advantage. Conclusion and future perspective

Our purposes are to examine that CSR activities lead to competitive advantage and sustainable development. These backgrounds are discussion about TBL, CSR and the expansion of SRI Market. TBL seemed to be new, but this is only an opportunity to revise or remind us essence of CSR which are already mentioned by some scholars. Of course, we need to have sense of TBL, because a realisation of the three sets of perspectives, sociality, environmental and economical is very important for thesociety. In stakeholder theory, it is assumed that all stakeholder of a firm is treated equally. This means that requirements of stakeholders regarded as equal. It is also assumed that there are explicit non-financial principal-agency relationship among a firm and stakeholder. So there are explicit contracts among them.

In SRI market, it is also observed that so many individuals who are interested in CSR activities of a firm or want to support it invest such a firm. And SRI market expands so large and has still growth potential. This means that not only return on investing SRI fund is rally good, but also so many investors are really interested in CSR activities. That expansion helps a firm which is not so big to finance.

Sociality, environmental and economical perspectives are treated equally on perspective of stakeholder theory. Social and environmental perspectives are not instruments to gain profits.

Environmental and social perspectives could be connected with core competence of a firm. Toyota has already suggested that and Body shop has also. These cases are landmark in markets and they play bottom line's role. If such a big firm like Toyota suggests a new type of strategy, other firms in same industry imitate its strategy or think other strategies to compete with Toyota in new market like eco market which is found by Toyota.

We examined how a firm manages CSR according to Toshiba's actual activities. Toshiba's example has showed us that Toshiba has already tackled CSR management with having a view of stakeholder theory and how it is important.

We need to suggest more empirical data and more cases to strengthen thearguments. First there are so many funds in SRI market. We have to develop rating system of CSR. Some articles suggests how to rate CSR. But a study of evaluation of SRI does not exist as far as we know, so we have to develop evaluation system of SRI funds. It does not handle its performance, but its rating system. Then we would like to compare SRI funds by using criteria and systems, which we will develop. So we could find the real world of SRI funds.

References

Bevan, D. (2008). *Continental Philosophy: A Grounded Theory Approach and the Emergence of Convenient and Inconvenient Ethics. Cutting Edge Issues in Business Ethics*. M. Painter-Morland and P. Werhane. Boston, Springer. 24: 131–152.

Drucker, P. (1981). "What is business ethics?" *The Public Interest Spring* (63). 18–36.

Koehn, D. (2002). *Ethical Issues in Human Resources. The blackwell guide to business ethics*. N. E. Bowie. Oxford, Blackwell: 225–243.

Lee, M. (2005). *Critiquing code of ethics. Critical Thinking in Human Resource Development*. C. Elliott and S. Turnbull. London, Routledge.

Machan, T. R. *Business ethics in a free society. A Companion To Business Ethics*. R. E. Frederic. Oxford, Blackwell: 88–99.

12

Competitive Analysis in Business

Competitive means that a contest is occurring between two or more parties. The sources of this can be multifaceted, originating in product or service offerings, shelf-space negotiations, supplier contracts, and investor relations, to name just a few. Usually, competitive bouts end up with a winner, and no further contest is needed. Competition here is about achieving a sustainable winning performance, not delivering one action that simply wounds, but consistently beating the rest who are working, most likely, toward the same or very similar goals as your enterprise.

Strategic is a word used today to describe almost every decision and/or action taken, when in reality there is a clear mix of the no less valuable, tactical decision making taking place. The generic use of a word such as "strategic" can diminish its real role and mask the impact that a true strategic decision has. Strategic decisions, as opposed to tactical, operational, or instantaneous decisions, have a unique set of characteristics to differentiate them. These distinctions occur along the dimensions of time, frequency, effort required, consequences, and impact. Strategic decisions typically:

— address at least a medium-term time horizon, at best long-term (time).

— occur infrequently or emerge from a formalised planning cycle (frequency).

— require significant input from key people (effort).

— require significant information input from key functions (effort).

— require substantial resources to formulate and implement (effort).
— affect the long-term direction of the organisation (consequences).
— affect many, if not all, of the organisation's activities (consequences).
— affect competitive dynamics (impact).
— involve major change to the firm's activities (impact).
— become the over-arching blueprint for subsequent decisions (impact).

If all or a significant number of the preceding elements are present, the greater the likelihood that the decision is indeed strategic. Many non-strategic decisions help to determine the performance of an enterprise in a marketplace, particularly in the shorter term. Decisions such as seasonal price discounting, direct mail campaigns, product enhancements, and ambush marketing are all examples of non-strategic decisions. They have a short-term lifespan and a short-term effect.

The key to our identification of a strategic decision is that they are the ones typically made by senior executives, managing directors, and/or the senior management team. Consequently, the enterprise that gets the strategic decisions "right" has a far greater chance of also getting the non-strategic decisions right.

Competitive analysis is the cornerstone of effective strategy formulation and execution. Valuable analysis helps decision makers to understand and predict critical market-changing actions that may be taken by competitors and other competition-impacting stakeholders. These decision makers are charged with answering a small number of very powerful questions about their organisation, including the following:

— What is our current status or situation?
— What are our options?
— Which direction do we want to go?
— Which direction should we go?
— How can we get to where we have decided we are going?
— How will we know that we have gotten there?

Like many developing fields of inquiry, business and competitive analysis is NOT purely art or science, but a combination of substantial portions of both in its effective application. As with the type of research formally taught to scientists, the analysis process can be viewed as holding much in common with the scientific method. Analysts will observe certain events, persons, or actions, develop a proposition or hypothesis that describes/ explains what they have observed, and then use the hypothesis to make predictions about what may subsequently occur. These predictions can then be further assessed through additional observations or data, and the hypotheses can be modified based on the results.

This process, which can be applied in theory by analysts, gets complicated very quickly by factors present in the real world of business and marketplace competition, as well as the politics and social nature of decision makers and enterprises. Analysts frequently work in groups or teams and benefit from the pooling of expertise. Hypotheses aren't always developed, tested, or reformulated, but are frequently modified in real-time by the evidence that is acquired. These factors point to genuine business and competitive analysis being more of a social scientific pursuit than that of physical or pure science.

The "real world" tends to bring out the "art" aspect of analysis. When conducting an experiment using control groups, we know that some percentage of a treatment group's analyses will not confirm the control group's analyses. Analysts in these two groups will weigh the same data or information differently, based on schemes that may be hard for others to accurately replicate. Even when analysts do substantively agree about the nature of the problems being addressed, they can still subsequently disagree about the proposed course of action. Consequently, analysts may never be able to "prove" they were right. It is these kinds of experiences that points to why analysis can sometimes be viewed as more akin to art than science. The following humorous parable helps point out some of the important differences between the two perspectives.

Business and competitive analysts are tasked with making sense out of often ambiguous, complex, and challenging matters that decision makers care about. Like the artist on the bus, they too have to weigh up the odds, work through the scenarios, work out what they know as opposed to their competition, and take action. They have to make sense of, or create meaning from, a typically constrained sample of data and information. In an often-confused and rapidly moving competitive landscape, they try to answer the three critical questions commonly asked of them:

— "What?"
— "So what?"
— "Now what?"

Any of these three questions may be answered in a variety of constructive ways using replicable procedures and methods (science), as well as intuitive or creative ones (art).

Importance of Intelligence

It is important to understand the place of intelligence within the larger context of an enterprise. The need to generate competitive intelligence (CI) is certainly not new. Sun Tzu plainly stated the rationale for intelligence over two thousand years ago. He wrote, "Now the reason the enlightened prince and the wise general conquer the enemy whenever they move, and their achievements surpass those of ordinary men, is foreknowledge."

Intelligence processes in business organisations have received significant attention in recent decades. The benefits gained by successfully anticipating a competitor's future plans and strategies are generally self-evident. The consequences of making decisions based on information that is incomplete, inaccurate, or late are as severe.

CI often engenders images of fictional secret agents such as James Bond using an impressive array of sophisticated gadgetry to eavesdrop on their business competition. In reality, CI can be exhilarating, but not because of illegal skullduggery. Modern CI practitioners are stimulated by using their unique set of skills, knowledge, abilities, and instincts to uncover relationships that enable their organisations to compete more effectively. Most CI practice includes a heavy dose of analytical capabilities. Analysts are prominent, central members of CI functions in today's successful, global enterprises.

There are numerous definitions of CI in contemporary practice and scholarship. Our current sense is that no single definition of CI is likely to be precise and universally accepted. As such, CI is generally viewed as the process by which organisations gather actionable information about competitors and the competitive environment and, ideally, apply it to their planning processes and decision-making in order to improve their enterprise's performance.

CI links signals, events, perceptions, and data into discernible patterns and trends concerning the business and competitive environment. CI can be simple scanning, such as analysing a company's annual report and other public documents, or elaborate, such as performing a fully digitised war gaming exercise. CI is not business espionage; it is ethical, legal, legitimate, and essential. Business espionage develops intelligence by illegal or cloak-and-dagger means such as breaking and entering, bribery, coercion, deliberate deception or advertising "phantom" job vacancies, electronic eavesdropping, bugging or tapping, network infiltration, or systems hacking. CI practitioners use public, but not necessarily published, information. In other words, the information the CI practitioner seeks is readily available and identified through legal means of open sources such as public documents, interviews, and in-house expertise. It does not involve the theft of trade secrets.

One way to understand CI is to view it as a progression from raw inputs to finished outputs. In this perspective, CI begins with scattered bits of raw, basic data. This raw material is then organised by CI practitioners and becomes information. Information becomes intelligence when it is placed into a format useful to a decision-maker's unique or critical intelligence needs (CINs). Using this lens, CI is the refined intelligence product produced by an analyst that meets a decision-maker's unique needs for understanding a competitive aspect of the internal and/or external environment. Effective CI helps the decision-maker make a better decision!

CI can also be viewed as an organisational function ranging in scope between the broader area of business intelligence (BI) and the narrower version practiced as competitor analysis (CA). A CI function provides the foundation on which strategy and tactics are built, assessed, and modified. As a mostly staff-oriented function, CI will cut across and overlap other functions, in particular, those associated with marketing, planning, and strategy.

Competitive Intelligence Programmes (CIPs) have goals such as proactively detecting opportunities or threats; eliminating or reducing blindspots, risks, and/or surprises; and reducing reaction time to competitor and marketplace changes. CIPs attempt to ensure that decision makers have accurate, current information about the organisation's competitive environment, and a plan for using that information.

Component in the Intelligence Cycle

Analysis is arguably that portion of the larger intelligence process in which the greatest value is generated. Much organisational experience suggests it can also be more difficult to do than the resource-draining data and information collection efforts that most organisations have emphasised in recent years.

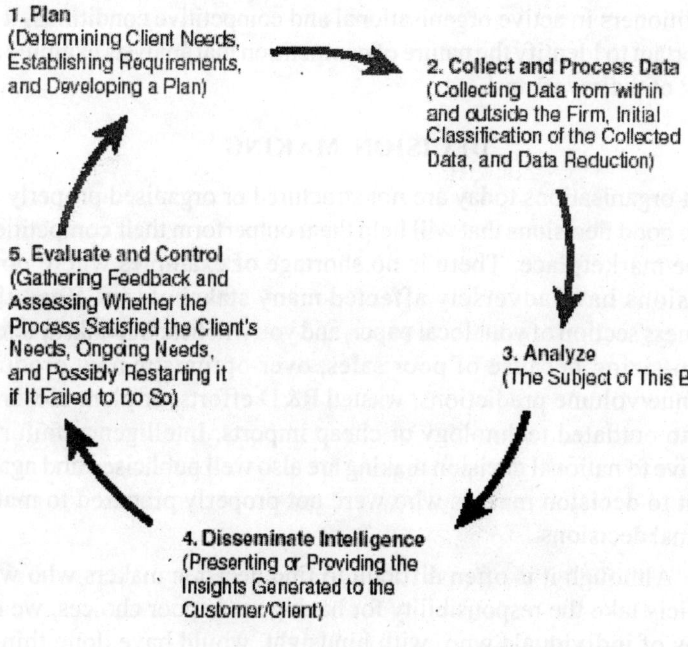

Figure 1. A generic intelligence cycle

Nevertheless, there is a long series of research and publications that suggests that business and competitive analysis serves a variety of important, long-standing needs for organisations. Analysis is just one step of a larger process for developing intelligence for an organisation. Most depictions of the so-called "intelligence cycle" show a series of 4 to 6 steps in a stripped-down form.

The analysis step in this cycle involves its own set of sub-tasks that need to be conducted in order to generate effective outputs and outcomes. Analysis works interactively with all the sub-processes of data classification and synthesis to produce a finished product such as a chart, graph, table, text, summary, visual, or other communicative aids appropriate for dissemination.

Analysis involves the skilful application of a variety of techniques. All of these will help decision makers make sense of intelligence. Intelligence analysis is always context-specific in that it does not occur within a vacuum, a static condition, or under experimental conditions. Because analysis is performed by practitioners in active organisational and competitive conditions, it is important to identify the nature of competition that analysts examine as a part of their work task.

DECISION MAKING

Most organisations today are not structured or organised properly to make good decisions that will help them outperform their competition in the marketplace. There is no shortage of examples where poor decisions have adversely affected many stakeholders. Read the business section of your local paper, and you will hear of bankruptcies, down-sizing because of poor sales, over-optimistic new product revenue/volume predictions, wasted R&D efforts, or plant closures due to outdated technology or cheap imports. Intelligence failures relative to national decision making are also well publicised and again point to decision makers who were not properly prepared to make optimal decisions.

Although it is often difficult to find decision makers who will publicly take the responsibility for having made poor choices, we all know of individuals who, with hindsight, would have done things differently. Today's managers face an abundance of information in their decision-making contexts, and sometimes this information abundance causes them to be paralysed. Benjamin Gilad notes how information arriving to top managers is invariably biased, subjective, filtered, and/or late. Analysts have the means for helping reduce both the volume and rate of this information flow while simultaneously assuring the quality of the product being delivered. They can then greatly enhance the executive's actual ability and confidence in effective decision making.

Analysis has been revitalised in the "knowledge" era, or the era of intellectual capital. Whatever we should call it, knowledge is increasingly recognised as a key organisational asset that can distinguish between the winners and losers in many competitive marketplaces. Organisations that can effectively generate, capture, disseminate, and apply knowledge better and faster than their competitors stand a higher probability of achieving successful performance. Analysts are a critical part of this knowledge-oriented process as they are among the primary directors of knowledge in an organisation. Analysts must provide direction and guidance to those individuals responsible for collecting data and information. They are the link to gathered data and the organisation's key decisions.

Analysis is just as important because of the increased recognition and value on good thinking skills. Analysis cannot be conducted in the absence of thinking. Without it, we would have random choice and luck. This is not the best foundation for a considered outcome and is increasingly likely to suffer from "extinction by instinct." The other end of the continuum is from "paralysis by analysis." That is not to summarily discount the value of instinct, but it has to be measured alongside more reliable and tested methods of analysis.

Competitors in Enterprises

Beating competitors, in many industries, has become a necessity rather than a desirable goal. More insightful strategy development and execution has been needed since even a decade ago. The following reasons are among the most critical ones underlying increased competition, all of which produce a greater need for improved business and competitive analysis.

— *Explosion of access to cheap and fast information*: Whether it is employee mobility, greater access to higher education in both traditional and on-line formats, companies showing less loyalty to their employees, or those same employees showing less loyalty to their employers, the window on competition and competitive opportunities has grown wider and more transparent. Because of changing information and communication technology, as well as changing sociocultural value systems, keeping key competitive information proprietary and out of the sight or hands of competitors has become more difficult than ever before.

— *Maturation of industries and businesses*: Many industries that were prominent in the twentieth century were resource-based industries, such as forest products, manufacturing, steel, and so on. These have rapidly matured or have seen a dramatic slowdown compared to past rates of growth. Many have struggled to institutionalise innovation capabilities, resources, strategies, new resource inputs, new production processes, new product development challenges, new employee skill recruitment and integration, new distribution channels, and/or understanding new customer needs. These are quite different challenges to simply trying to build market share in an existing static and simple market space, and the potential for them to miss the disruptive forms of activity that may be occurring on the fringes of their still-lucrative markets is high.

— *Loss of traditional means of competitive structuring and advantage:* Traditionally, companies could achieve competitive advantage through scale economies, segment entrenchment, first-mover advantages, and other such industry level gains. While still existing in some sectors, these approaches are now so quickly and easily imitated that they no longer deliver sustainable advantage. While the generic strategies of cost, differentiation, and focus described by Michael Porter are still conceptually fruitful, they are hard to achieve and sustain in practice. In a later paper, Porter himself reconsidered the traditional approaches and concluded that the achievement of advantage is positioning, rather than resource-based.

— *Sophisticated and better-informed consumers*: Customers are better informed than ever before and have access to significantly more information on which to base their purchasing decisions. As with B2B markets, buying habits are less ingrained, and purchases are increasingly based on specification, cost, and value. Today's consumer is less likely to be swayed by an emotional appeal and will do hard-nosed research before striking a deal, especially with big ticket items.

Companies that still think they can sell anything they like, at any price, to a gullible customer may well do so once, but not again. Bad news travels fast, and the presence of customer pressure groups, Internet blogs, and vociferous word-of-mouth channels will quickly damage a brand.

— *Dynamic and rapidly evolving technology*: Physical strengths are being replaced by intangible assets such as intellectual property, knowledge, intelligence, brands, R&D teams, and market position, resulting in volume-based advantages being less prominent. Even in industries where scale-based advantages still exist, typically manufacturing, the continual push by businesses across the globe to improve operational efficiency has made it harder to sustain such advantages. This has made the development of effectiveness-based strategy and execution more critical than ever.

There is little doubt that competition compels organisations to respond, preferably in a proactive manner. Designing these responses and assessing their impact are the primary task of the business and competitive analyst. The context within which the analysis is undertaken and the organisation within which the analyst is working, will, inevitably, produce unique demands.

IMPROVIN G BBUSINESS PERFORMANCE

Business enterprises today are expected to meet standards of responsible business conduct that go beyond what had been expected traditionally. Although people more often than not still speak of business in terms of products, jobs, and profits, it is understood and accepted across the globe that a business enterprise remains a member of its community. The pursuit of profits and economic progress is not a license to ignore community norms, values, and standards of respect, integrity, and quality.

Improved business performance, profits, and economic progress come to those who effectively and efficiently foster and meet the reasonable expectations of their primary stakeholders-customers, employees, suppliers, investors, and the environment, as well as the owners and managers themselves. Success for any business is ultimately measured in profits and losses, and the socially responsible business generates the capital and revenues required to operate and stay in business over the long haul. The socially responsible business must generate enough revenue to cover the real cost of capital, the risks and uncertainties of future economic activity, and the needs of its workers and pensioners. The socially irresponsible enterprise, however, fails to cover these costs because it is unable to meet the reasonable expectations of its stakeholders.

For example, an effective, efficient, and responsible enterprise generates revenue by satisfying customers. It attracts capital by meeting investor expectations for return on investment. It increases effectiveness by attracting the best employees. It reduces costs by reducing mistakes, misconduct, and misunderstandings.

An Responsible Business Enterprises (RBE) holds some enduring purpose beyond profit to define the enterprise and inspire and guide its employees and agents, because a purpose beyond profit sustains business enterprises. Enterprise purpose, moreover, helps employees and agents have a deeper understanding of the intent behind specific goals, measures, and actions. "With this understanding," one author notes, "comes a greater acceptance of and, if they are consistent with the person's values, commitment to the individual goals."

An RBE is characterised by responsible business conduct at all four levels of its identity as an enterprise:

— Compliance with the law

— Risk management

— Reputation enhancement

— Value added to the community

Responsible business conduct includes the choices and actions of owners, managers, employees, and agents that are (a) within their authority, (b) well informed, (c) intended to pursue the enterprise purpose and meet reasonable stakeholder expectations, and (d) sustainable over time. Responsible business conduct allows an enterprise to improve its business performance, make profits, and contribute to the economic progress of its community.

Among the lessons learned by both business and government is that responsible business conduct can be encouraged by the structures and systems, procedures, and practices of responsible business conduct, often called good corporate governance or best practices. Moreover, many businesses now account for the impact they have on all their stakeholders, including their social impact-how they deal with employees, suppliers, and the community and their environmental impact-how they treat the environment.

A management tool owners and managers use to encourage responsible business conduct is commonly called a business ethics programme. A business ethics programme also helps owners and managers address the triple bottom line: the financial, social, and environmental results or impacts of the business's operations. Business owners and managers have learned that a business ethics programme helps owners and managers improve their business performance, make profits, and contribute to economic progress by better

— Recognising political, economic, social, and technological pressures Understanding organisational culture: core beliefs, participation, responsibility, knowledge sharing, and methods of dealing with conflict
— Fostering reasonable stakeholder expectations Developing responsible management practices to meet stakeholder expectations
— Learning from enterprise decisions and activities

Responsible Business Global Marketplace

The market economy has become increasingly global. Leaders in business, government, and nongovernmental organisations (NGOs) now see global economic development as "the best way to increase prosperity within and among countries, and to create opportunities for millions of people, especially in the developing world, to secure a decent life for themselves and their children." The challenge is to find the right balance between emerging global norms, values, and standards and local cultures, business practices, and community needs.

Businesses in emerging market economies face many challenges. For example, although no society approves of paying or accepting bribes, in societies where workers receive lower than subsistence-level pay, "expediting fees" (also known as "bribes") often become unapproved but accepted behaviour under local custom. In such societies, bribery is so common that even law enforcement officials pay bribes to gain their positions.

The programme must recognise that management policies, standards, and procedures will be open to interpretation at all levels of the enterprise. For example, a superficial approach to responsible business conduct condemns bribes and threatens to punish those who pay or accept them. However, a business ethics programme takes a comprehensive approach. It recognises such accepted behaviour as part of the challenges facing the enterprise and addresses such issues systemically. In other words, it addresses them at their roots by examining hiring processes, compensation schemes, and training and education; by instituting monitoring, auditing, and reporting mechanisms; and by influencing the legislative or regulatory processes.

A business ethics programme does not set up either the enterprise or its employees and agents for failure. Rather, it strives to place the right people in the right positions in the enterprise to foster and meet reasonable stakeholder expectations as the surest means to improved business performance, profits, and economic progress. It scans the relevant context of the enterprise and its organisational culture to identify challenges and to develop responsible ways to meet them. It starts from the assumption that enterprises are integral parts of their communities. It encourages them to work within the community to overcome the challenges of emerging market economies and contribute to community-driven development.

Moreover, a business ethics programme takes care not to mistake cultural, legal, or religious differences for a lack of ethics. In Islamic countries, for example, mudaraba (reflecting a Sharia law requirement that a lender charge no interest) may result in forms of payment that could be mistaken by those unfamiliar with the culture as inappropriate or unethical (that is, as "kickbacks"). A common cultural difference is the attitude toward hiring relatives. In some cultures, it is expected that owners and managers will hire relatives as a matter of course. In others, hiring relatives, which is known as nepotism, is discouraged or, in some circumstances, prohibited.

As long as businesses concentrate their attention and efforts on dealing with everyday challenges rather than striving to rise above them, they may be part of the problem. For example, although paying a small bribe to get a permit or to evade taxes may be "just the way things are done" or something that "everyone does," businesses that do so may perpetuate business practices and conduct that make the evolution to a market economy more difficult. The ultimate issue for an RBE in an emerging market economy is whether it sees itself as part of the current problem or part of the solution.

Medium-sized Enterprise

The "place business should occupy in society" is a particularly challenging issue for the small to medium-sized enterprise (SME). Each SME is unique, often taking on the character of its owners and managers. There is surprisingly little research into the social responsibility of the SME. Moreover, it is difficult, at best, to generalise the SME experience from country to country or even between regions within a particular country.

SMEs in emerging markets are pioneers; they are plowing new ground as they contribute to developing a market economy. In most economies, they provide the bulk of jobs, especially new jobs, and contribute significantly to the welfare of their communities because they are so closely connected. However, SMEs often lack the capital, staff, or time of large, complex enterprises (LCEs) to address many business issues. For example, tracking and complying with changing laws and regulations are relatively more costly for SMEs. SMEs seldom have the close relationships with government that LCEs have, especially those recently privatised. They are often unable to defend themselves against unreasonable decrees, laws, or regulations or to advocate for changes that would facilitate the transition to a market economy.

Though many of the best practices developed over the past two decades reflect the experiences of LCEs, there are a number of reasons why an SME might profit by adapting what the LCEs have learned:

— The SME of today is more apt to become the LCE of tomorrow by adopting emerging global standards and adapting the best practices of successful LCEs.
— By adopting global standards and adapting best practices where they make sense, owners and managers are able to distinguish their SME from the competition.
— By understanding the basic principles and practices of the emerging global marketplace, owners and managers will be better able to recognise responsible business conduct issues earlier and to work with others to find solutions.
— Especially in a business environment that some perceive as high risk, first impressions count. Developing a business ethics programme will help owners and managers present a core set of beliefs and standards more clearly, thus demonstrating to investors and customers their enterprise's commitment to being an RBE in the global marketplace.
— If an SME's people are conversant in the language of emerging global standards and best practices, they will be better able to speak the language of the global markets-and the opportunities to be found there.

Whereas the process of developing standards, procedures, and expectations is the same for all enterprises, the answers for each enterprise will depend on the size and complexity of the enterprise itself. The goal for the SME is not to duplicate the standards, procedures, infrastructure, practices, and expectations of LCEs, but to learn from them-and to improve them. Moreover, SMEs will find that they need not act alone in adopting the world-class standards, procedures, infrastructure, practices, and expectations described in these materials. Chambers of commerce, business associations, colleges and universities, NGOs, and other professional advisers can use the guide to help SMEs find their way.

For the enterprise in an emerging market economy struggling to make payroll, not to mention a profit, global economic development is, at once, an opportunity, a risk, and a challenge. As an opportunity, it offers tantalising prospects for new markets and access to international capital. The risk, however, is heightened competition and capital flow reversals from the slightest perceived political, economic, or social threat. The challenge is to learn from the experiences of successful businesses in market economies and to adapt them to overcome the legacies of the command economy. By learning from others' experiences (including the mistakes), enterprises in emerging markets can contribute to the development of their own market economies and can join the global marketplace.

A business can influence-but not control-the political, economic, and social contexts in which it operates (its relevant context). Business leaders must work with NGOs and government legislators and regulators to develop a political, economic, and social context in which responsible businesses can compete fairly-and succeed. Businesses and societies that do not meet or aspire to meet these global standards and expectations are unlikely to be ready to participate fully in the global marketplace.

Central Planning and State-owned Production

Central planning and state-owned production characterised command economies. Resources were allocated by plan instead of by markets. Employment was generally full but effectively rationed through an internal passport system. Capital was allocated centrally through a single institution. Enterprises were responsible for production but not for marketing or pricing. Since planning was based on quantity, not quality, enterprises had little incentive for innovation; indeed, innovation or quality improvement was often punished with higher quotas or standards.

The law restricted or abolished human and property rights and the sanctity of contract. It limited individual rights rather than state power. The legal system lacked procedural and institutional tools to protect individual property and human rights and support the sanctity of contract. The legislative framework was not oriented toward private enterprise, and regulators, judges, and lawyers had little knowledge of, or experience in, free market concepts.

When governments abruptly halted central planning of an entire economy, they left a legacy of cultural, institutional, and economic hurdles for marketoriented reform. The networks of business relationships that form the core of a market economy were largely nonexistent, and enterprises had to develop them without the benefit of markets and supportive institutional and legal frameworks.

Economic Competition

The competition and innovation to meet the most important needs of customers and consumers, which characterise a market economy, were either unlawful or discouraged in command economies. For relative ease of control, state-owned enterprises tended to be large. New, competitive firms were few and were found more often in the unofficial or "shadow economy." Even state-owned enterprises survived through an informal bartering system, which remains, in large part, to this day. Exit-that is, failure-was seldom feasible because the economy was expected to maintain full employment and because of the official embarrassment that would arise from a failure. There was little competition from foreign producers, since trade relations were governed and restricted by planners.

In many emerging market economies, it is still relatively difficult for a firm to enter the market. The number of procedures, time of entry, and cost of entry vary, but they often greatly exceed what is required to set up an enterprise in a market economy. Enterprises are still expected to provide work and housing to some extent. When the high costs of entry are combined with low levels of "latent entrepreneurship" (an individual preference for self-employment as opposed to employment), domestic competitive forces develop slowly, and open markets become less an opportunity than a threat.

Contact with Stakeholders

In a command economy, individual enterprises rarely had direct contact with suppliers, customers, or consumers-some of the stakeholders in a business enterprise. For many owners and managers, the concept of a stakeholder is novel, even strange. Entrepreneurs now have to develop these essential relationships, and many others, where none existed before:

— *Customers and consumers*. Recently privatised enterprises had to shift their attention and efforts from satisfying the express preferences of planners-especially in heavy industry-to identifying and satisfying the preferences of customers and consumers.

— *Employees and agents*. In a centrally planned economy, where the quantity of goods produced is more important than their quality or fitness for customer purpose, managers could afford to look at employees as "hands." Independent judgment was often discouraged, and objectivity was seldom valued. People were not expected to bring unique qualities to their jobs. Indeed, until relatively recently, industrial economies saw employees much the same way. In today's market economies, however, a business enterprise needs to tap all the human potential available to it to compete effectively. Enterprises now recognise that they must invest in their employees and agents and "create a work environment that respects the dignity and contribution of each individual."

— *Suppliers and service providers. With* the abolition of central planning, an enterprise needs to develop a chain of suppliers, since it can now choose what suppliers and service providers it wants to work with-and vice versa.

— *Shareholders and owners*. Often, the privatisation methods used by many transitioning economies failed to ensure the presence of a strategic owner: a single shareholder with sufficient stake to provide motivation for monitoring management effectively. Conversely, some voucher privatisation schemes resulted in abusive corporate takeovers whereby an individual was able to purchase small shares of a major state asset at a low cost and to take control of that asset through abuse of the legal process and through corrupt practices. In either event, privatisation schemes often failed to require effective corporate governance systems. Where there is separation of ownership and management without accountability, there is little incentive for managers to make decisions to the benefit of shareholders who have no voice. Managers are, in such cases, able to use the assets of the enterprise to their own purposes.

— *Lenders and investors*. Since in a command economy success for an enterprise was measured by meeting production quotas, businesses had little or no experience with the risk management aspects of lending and investing. Corporate governance encouraging financial transparency is developing slowly, but a continuing barter system makes financial analysis for capital and credit difficult.

— *Government officials and agencies*. Under a command economy, the political system fundamentally favoured incumbent firms. At the local level, relationships were very close between politicians or bureaucrats and senior management. Though most state enterprises have by now been privatised, many of these close relationships between politicians and business managers remain in place.

In some societies, many large enterprises strive to "capture" the state by securing the passage of laws or by obtaining licenses that benefit them over other enterprises. In others, the state has effectively captured the economy by controlling a dominant crop or natural resource, for example, even though economic resources are nominally owned by the private sector.

Law of Business

A market economy requires a high degree of confidence in the rule of law for business to meet its economic, social, and environmental responsibilities. In many emerging market economies, the vast majority of people do not trust one another. The distrust surrounding the enforceability of contracts, for example, leads to large portions of the population believing that negotiations are not over even after a contract is signed. Transaction costs to protect one party from the other in such circumstances are much higher as a result.

A legal framework oriented toward free markets and reliable judicial institutions is essential for this confidence to develop over time. Such a framework will need:

— Contract laws

— Laws regarding the formation, operation, management, and dissolution of corporations

— Laws on privatisation
— Real estate laws
— Laws against unfair competition
— Labour-management laws
— Tax laws
— Accounting and auditing standards
— Laws protecting intellectual property rights
— Bankruptcy laws
— Environmental protection legislation and regulation
— Laws ensuring fiduciary responsibilities of managers and directors
— Rules governing the rights and obligations of shareholders, managers, and boards of directors
— Laws permitting class-action suits

A confusing, burdensome, or even unfair legislative and regulatory framework drives up the cost of setting up a business, dissuades investors, and provides a fertile ground for corruption. As one researcher observes, "Some critics even believe that regulations are intentionally drafted in a confusing manner to provide officials with more discretion." Such a framework is particularly damaging to the SME. Under such circumstances, responsible business conduct is frequently discarded in favour of survival, or the law is bent or interpreted to fit the circumstances.

Even where laws and regulations are well drafted, they are often enforced unevenly-or ignored by the population-in practice. The failure to enforce the legislative and regulatory framework, or to comply with it, contributes to confusion, places the law-abiding enterprise at a competitive disadvantage, discourages investors, and extends a climate of corruption.

A key to introducing ethics in an emerging market economy, then, is to build a marketoriented legal framework and reliable judicial institutions. Prescriptive rules, which would be undue government interference in a developed economy, may be necessary to ensure that responsible business conduct becomes a norm, a value, and a standard. The RBE works with other leaders to influence government regulation to that end.

No less important than new laws, one researcher notes, is a judiciary proficient at interpreting and enforcing the law with integrity. The creation of effective dispute resolution mechanisms that can offer businesses transparent, predictable, and cost-effective results is one of the most important steps a government can take to support market processes in an emerging market economy. Finally, government agencies must exercise their authority and responsibility to execute the judgments reached.

A final legacy of central planning is a climate of illegal activity. This legacy stems from the autocratic nature of the state and the unaccountability of its officials in a command economy, the remaining close ties between government and business, the incomplete legal and institutional reforms, the political and economic instability, and the ineffective implementation of marketoriented reforms.

Among the consequences of a command economy was the emergence of an unofficial or "shadow economy," which was, by definition, unlawful. Current entry barriers increase the potential for administrative corruption, where entrepreneurs are tempted to pay bribes to overcome administrative barriers. Higher entry costs are associated with higher corruption and larger unofficial sectors of the economy.

With the collapse of central planning and the lack of external constraints, insiders and managers during the transition to a market economy often took the opportunity to appropriate state-owned enterprises for their benefit, leading to asset stripping and rent diversion. Often, important natural resources or whole industrial sectors were converted by insiders and managers.

Marketoriented Institutions

To raise the living standards of its people, a society must provide the conditions for a functioning market. In a free market, the role of government in the marketplace is limited to protecting it from those who would attack or abuse it. "The state creates and preserves the environment in which the market can safely operate." A free market minimises the role of command and maximises the scope for exchange of goods and service to meet important needs through transactions free of duress and not otherwise unconscionable. A suitable institutional framework for a market economy would typically contain at least the following seven components:

— A transparent regulatory system, including securities regulation
— A sophisticated accounting and banking profession
— A stock exchange with meaningful listing standards
— Labour-management regulations
— A system of protection for intellectual property
— Effective legal and judiciary systems
— A broad-based tax system

Emerging market economies are struggling to provide these conditions to overcome the legacies of central planning, but institutional development takes time to design and implement. How successful an emerging economy is at developing an institutional framework depends, at least in part, on whether (and how long) it had been a sovereign state, how well developed its institutions of public administration were, and how many valuable natural resources it can privatise. In the meantime, many owners and managers struggle with the question, "What does it mean to be a responsible business?" It is a sign of a healthy dialogue that leaders in businesses, governments, and civil society are asking the same question, not just in emerging market economies, but also across the globe.

INDIVIDUAL BUSINESS

The RBE recognises its many roles and responsibilities in the community-and engages its stakeholders-adding as much value as possible. Through creativity, flexibility, and responsiveness in its day-to-day operations, it can add value to the community in many ways:

— *Serving the most important needs of its customers and consumers*
Providing gainful employment for its employees and agents, so that they can provide for their families and be responsible citizens

  — Providing an adequate return to investors
  — Purchasing goods and services from its suppliers and service providers
  — Competing intensely, but fairly responsible business

- — Forming strategic partnerships and alliances to create new business opportunities
- — Supporting community infrastructure through taxes and fees
- — Participating in the political process to improve market conditions

— *Respecting the environment* :The trust-engendering manner in which an RBE engages its stakeholders is a substantial contribution to the community in and of itself. Such enterprises help lay a foundation for a functioning market economy for all.

In an emerging market economy, an RBE must confront and rise above the legacies of a command economy. As a part of the solution to its economy's problems, it can participate in three essential ways: improving its business performance; helping build social capital in its economy; and working with leaders in business, government, and civil society to develop the essential marketoriented legal framework and reliable judicial institutions.

Business Performance

An essential contribution of any business enterprise in the evolution to a market economy is to improve its own business performance. For all business enterprises, this is the first step toward making profits and contributing to economic progress. Performance can be improved by expanding and better engaging stakeholders as follows:

- — Establishing clear standards and procedures to guide employees and agents
- — Focusing on anticipating and meeting the needs and desires of customers and consumers more effectively and efficiently
- — Attracting, hiring, and bringing out the best in employees, suppliers, and service providers
- — Establishing internal control mechanisms to build confidence among dispersed owners and investors
- — Developing and maintaining strategic alliances with enterprises sharing the same values

These best practices are at the heart of a business ethics programme. They can help an enterprise improve its reputation, manage its risk, protect itself from its own employees and agents, strengthen its competitive position, expand its access to capital and credit, increase profits, sustain long-term growth, and gain international respect.

Building Social Capital

Respect, shared values, and mutual trust among individuals, businesses, NGOs, and government officials are the foundation of a market economy. To compete effectively and sustain economic growth, enterprises need social capital as well as financial capital. To contribute to this social capital, an RBE can

- Make the case in its community for a market economy and the role of responsible business.
- Develop a reputation for meeting the reasonable expectations of its stakeholders.
- Agree to voluntary forms of alternative dispute resolution, such as mediation and arbitration, while domestic courts are formed.
- Take responsibility for its mistakes and misconduct.
- Be willing to be held accountable for its mistakes and misconduct.
- Correct misunderstandings about its decisions and activities.
- Compete fairly with competition, both foreign and domestic.

How effectively, efficiently, and responsibly an enterprise is able to add value to its community depends, in large part, on how much its stakeholders trust one another. It may be that in markets and communities, especially in emerging market economies, the value an RBE most profitably adds is to be worthy of trust-and to encourage other market participants and community members to be trustworthy as well.

Leaders in Business

An RBE helps government create the conditions for a market economy by promoting responsible business conduct-through self-regulation or by conducting a public dialogue with government officials and NGOs. Even where the legal framework of decrees, laws, and regulations is unfair, supporting the rule of law is an important practice for an RBE.

Faced with an unfair legal framework, for example, businesses can work with other businesses and NGOs to point out the ethical dimensions of the decree, law, or regulation and to work for change.

Responsible businesses can serve as a voice for the community. They can work with leaders in government, business, and NGOs to do the following:

— Help develop the necessary institutional and legal frameworks for a market economy.
— Support initiatives to develop good public governance on the part of government itself.
— Strengthen NGOs to provide community-building services that business and government are unable to provide.

In economies where the government is unable to provide the social services a community requires, an RBE can work with other businesses and NGOs to identify community needs and can work with community-based organisations to provide such services. For example, the RBE can contribute supplies or services as a part of community-driven development, or it can contribute funds to community foundations. Some enterprises create their own charity programmes or foundations or support volunteer work by employees.

Management of Business Enterprise

It explores how a business ethics programme helps the responsible business enterprise (RBE) improve its business performance; help build social capital in its economy; and work with leaders in business, government, and civil society to develop a market framework and the supporting legal infrastructure. It examines specific sets of global standards and best practices of business ethics programmes, and it concludes with eight questions that responsible owners and managers must ask themselves for their enterprise.

There is much support for the notion that the discipline of responsible business conduct outlined here contributes to improving business performance and expanding opportunities for growth. Principal benefits coming to an enterprise that implements a business ethics programme are:

— Enhanced reputation and goodwill
— Reduced risks
— Reduced costs
— Protection from unethical employees and agents
— Enhanced performance, productivity, and competitive position
— Expanded access to capital, credit, and foreign investment
— Increased profits and sustained long-term growth
— Increased international respect

An enterprise's reputation for integrity is important for securing the loyalty of customers, for recruiting and retaining the most professional and honest employees, for becoming the business partner of choice, for winning local community acceptance, and for increasing access to capital and credit.

A business ethics programme contributes to the enterprise's reputation for integrity. By giving adequate guidance to employees and agents, it ensures that they know what is responsible business conduct. By helping form reasonable expectations among its stakeholders, it minimises disputes with customers and other stakeholders and increases stakeholder satisfaction.

Reduced Risks

Every business, even if it strives to comply strictly with the law, is subject to risks such as these:

— Being exposed to criminal prosecution for bribing a government contracting officer
— Being debarred from government contracting or a strategic partnership for an inappropriate gift or gratuity
— Having to recall products for failure to follow quality standards and procedures
— Having to clean up spills of toxic waste
— Dealing with employee claims of sexual harassment
— Dealing with lost employee time for health and safety problems
— Being placed on a blacklist of international, national, or local organisations

An RBE develops processes with which it identifies, assesses, and manages the full range of factors that might pose a risk to social and financial performance. The processes include assessing risks, establishing adequate standards and procedures, training, and monitoring and auditing systems. These processes help owners and managers plan, organise, and control the day-today operations of an enterprise to minimise risks to its capital, earnings, and reputation. They include management of risks associated with accidental losses, as well as operational risks such as those arising from financial mismanagement, fraud and embezzlement, corruption, and loss of reputation.

By providing employees clear guidelines on how to conduct day-to-day business in compliance with laws and ethics through a business ethics programme, the RBE can reduce transaction costs. A business ethics programme institutes procedures to detect and to prevent violations of the law and ethics. It provides employees with clear guidelines on a host of day-to-day transactions: how to conduct bids and tenders; how to conclude contracts; how to use confidential information; how to avoid conflicts of interest; and how to work with customers, suppliers, service providers, and competitors.

The cost of bribery, kickbacks, and other forms of illegal or corrupt conduct is not only the amount paid. The full cost includes management effort to allocate time to work with officials, to maintain a second set of books, and to deal with the threat of extortion and blackmail. The real cost is the risk to reputation and pride in the enterprise and the reduced prospects for participating in a market economy.

Unethical Employees and Agents

It is not pleasant to contemplate, but the enterprise itself is often abused by its employees and agents. Embezzlement of enterprise funds is a major example. Cheating on time cards or carrying off supplies and tools, while relatively minor, add up to significant losses sustained every year by businesses-both large and small. It has been estimated that enterprises in the United States lose some 6 percent of their revenues annually to employee misconduct.

A business ethics programme is designed to establish standards and procedures to prevent and detect violations of the trust put in employees. Among these standards and procedures are processes to protect enterprise assets. These specific processes may include establishing standards and procedures, monitoring and auditing systems, and reporting mechanisms.

However, at the heart of a business ethics programme is the desire of owners and managers to foster the commitment of their employees to the welfare of the enterprise as a whole. Fostering this sense of loyalty and commitment among employees and agents may be the most effective way in which a business ethics programme protects the enterprise from disloyal employees.

Productivity and Competitive Position

An RBE increases effectiveness and efficiency by enabling all stakeholders to work together closely on the basis of respect, shared values, and mutual trust. Such efforts lead to what one author calls "invisible savings" by reducing employee conduct that is harmful to the enterprise but difficult to detect. After a business ethics programme becomes a part of operations, many of the costs of monitoring and supervision can be reduced.

Product quality may improve and transaction costs, such as contracting, may decline. For example, many large, complex enterprises (LCEs), most of which have business ethics programmes, are developing preferred supplier lists to reduce the number of suppliers that they deal with. To ensure that there is no interruption in supplies and services, these LCEs require that their supply chains adopt the same good management practices that they follow, including a business ethics programme.

Since, in the minds of most employees, ethics are essentially a matter of fairness, a business ethics programme often increases employee morale. Better morale leads to increased productivity and innovation. It strengthens the enterprise's competitive position in its industry.

A business ethics programme, including aggressive risk management processes, may increase an RBE's attractiveness to investors. Before making loans, international lending institutions and domestic banks perform due diligence on whether an enterprise is managed well. They look to see whether an enterprise has strong financial supervision and internal controls. A business ethics programme is designed to prevent and detect illegal and unethical practices. Financial institutions may view management as a worthy credit risk and allow access to capital at lower rates.

When entering new markets, foreign investors seek reliable partners who demonstrate integrity and operate on a transparent basis. A business ethics programme reflecting global norms and values provides a common language between an enterprise and foreign investors. It creates opportunity to build partnerships that are based on respect, shared values, and mutual trust.

The discipline of responsible business conduct does not deliver instant results. However, a business ethics programme-including infrastructure and processes for continuous monitoring of compliance with law and ethics-should help an enterprise be more reliable and stable over time. Once an RBE has demonstrated its ability to detect and to prevent violations of the law and ethics, it tends to earn stakeholder confidence. This confidence leads to an increase in the value of shares; to wider access to capital and credit; to new clients, customers, and partners; and to further opportunities for expansion.

Adhering to the discipline of responsible business conduct can help enterprises gain access to international markets. It encourages compliance with laws and regulations that require a high level of transparency. When the generally accepted business practices of a community are based on sound standards and reasonable expectations, fair competition is the norm and the RBE can operate on a level playing field. Fair competition may encourage trading partners to reduce trade barriers such as tariffs and quotas.

Recent research suggests that a business ethics programme is particularly valuable in times of merger, acquisition, and restructuring. It is thought that the essential elements of a business ethics programme may help members of often distinct organisational cultures manage their differences until they find common ground. These elements include core beliefs, standards, and procedures; high-level personnel responsible for the programme; and dedicated resources to help employees seek advice. Enterprises undergoing privatisation should also consider the advantages of a business ethics programme as a means to reduce the risks associated with this transition process.

Social Capital

To define an RBE's social responsibility, we can think in terms of levels of social responsibility and try to appreciate the role of business in generating social capital. Thinking in terms of levels-social responsibility and ultrasocial responsibility-reminds us that if a business were to do no more than accomplish its essential business purpose of meeting the important needs of its customers, it would still be making a significant contribution to the common good. Appreciating the role of business in generating social capital confirms the stake that an RBE has in its communities and reaffirms the essential social value of responsible business.

The essential function of any business is to identify and meet the most important needs of its customers. In a free market, it is only by serving customers well that the enterprise will survive and prosper over time. An RBE is an essential part of a market economy, serving the needs of customers while making a profit for its owners and investors. It does so by cooperating well with its primary stakeholders-employees, suppliers, service providers, and investors-as well as many others.

By entering the marketplace, an RBE does not cease to be a member of its community. Being in business is not a license to ignore community norms, values, and standards. An RBE uses good judgment in evaluating the social impact of its goods and services on customers and the community as a whole. For example, although it may be legal to sell a product such as tobacco or alcohol, an RBE will not sell to minors, who may abuse the product. This practice is known as "socially responsible business."

The socially responsible business works hard and competes fairly. It recognises that to destroy the fabric of a marketplace to make a profit is shortsighted. It does not abuse the public trust or degrade the environment, which we all rely on. These principles are captured in the following definition of corporate social responsibility:

> A new business strategy in which companies conduct business responsibly by contributing to the economic health and sustainable development of the communities in which they operate, offer employees healthy, safe, and rewarding work conditions, offer quality, safe products, and service... are accountable to stakeholders... and provide a fair return to shareholders whilst fulfilling the above principles.

As a participant in markets and a member of its community, the socially responsible business expresses its needs and concerns to government when appropriate. It avoids using its economic power to gain competitive advantage through political means.

Although the essential purpose of an RBE is to improve its business performance, to return a profit to its owners and investors, and to increase the prosperity of its community by meeting the reasonable expectations of its stakeholders, the RBE is nevertheless concerned about the quality of life in its communities. Its employees and agents also care about the communities in which they and their families live.

Businesses often support literacy programmes, local schools and colleges, and local infrastructure, such as water facilities, roads, or parks. They may benefit from these as members of their communities. Supporting literacy programmes and education, for example, may lead to better employee applicants. Moreover, in some communities, a socially responsible business is expected or required to contribute a certain percentage of its income to institutions caring for the poor and needy.

In other communities, enterprises support such programmes because such involvement makes stakeholders feel better about themselves and the enterprise. For example, one enterprise recently developed a programme supporting research on dolphins in the Persian Gulf. Through that contribution to the community, the enterprise not only enhanced its reputation, but also gave great pride to its employees.

Some people confuse this sense of social responsibility with what it means to be a socially responsible business. Nothing could be further from the truth. The important point to remember is that a business is socially responsible simply by virtue of effectively, efficiently, and responsibly meeting the reasonable expectations of its stakeholders.

Trust and Social Capital

Responsible business, as an essential part of a free market, is an investment in growth for a country as well as for an enterprise. Trust cannot be imposed; it must be earned. The RBE makes a singular contribution to the community by positioning itself so that it is able to pursue its purpose as an enterprise over the long run, meeting the most important needs of its customers.

Social capital is "performance-based trust." It is "the ability of people to work together for common purposes in groups and organisations." Each participant in a market or society is responsible for contributing to the pattern of reasonable expectations. In such a community, trust will be rewarded. The RBE strives to be a trustworthy member of its community in order to contribute to its social capital.

Social capital is the foundation of a successful market economy. The benefits of operating in a high-trust environment are many. As one scholar observes, "A high-trust society can organise its workplace on a more flexible and group-oriented basis, with more responsibility delegated to lower levels of the organisation. Low-trust societies, by contrast, must fence in and isolate their workers with a series of bureaucratic rules."

Another scholar lists eight studies that demonstrate the link between values in general, trust in particular, and profitability. The link is based on an increase in creativity, support of management decisions, knowledge sharing, and pride, among other factors. A climate of trust can be abused, however. Customers who are not attentive may purchase goods or services of poor quality. Employees may steal from their employers. Government agents may take advantage of an enterprise that goes to them for aid. Indeed, it is precisely because people put trust in others that many irresponsible business practices are possible.

The discipline of responsible business conduct described in this manual leads owners and managers to build their enterprises with structures and systems that will compensate for a lack (or abuse) of trust. Over time, such conduct will lead to an organisational culture that is based on shared values and practices; more trust among stakeholders; and more effective, efficient, and profitable performance.

Government and Civil Society

Social capital also accrues through the efforts of civil society: organisations, such as trade groups, business associations, service clubs, charities, university faculty, and other nongovernmental organisations (NGOs) that aim to hold business and government officials accountable. Business enterprises, in general, have the potential to be powerful and influential members of their communities.

The RBE helps create the conditions for good public governance by promoting responsible business conduct-through self-regulation or through public dialogue with government officials. These forms of voluntary action help build social capital-the trust and shared values among individuals, government officials, civil society, the local community, and business that make it possible to work together on a cooperative basis.

Though a business enterprise is often portrayed as an isolated entity doing whatever it can to make a profit, the enterprise, whether large or small, is an integral part of its market, its community, and its society. As such, the social responsibilities of a business are to improve its performance, to make profits, and to increase the prosperity of its community by meeting the reasonable expectations of its stakeholders.

Responsible business conduct addresses the issues of ethics, compliance with laws and regulations, and social responsibility. Businesses face these issues every day in a market economy. This manual sees responsible business conduct as a discipline, as something responsible owners and managers can build on, and as an integral part of good management practice. Approaching responsible business conduct as a discipline broadens the thought processes of owners and managers by addressing the issues raised by business and professional ethics, organisational ethics, corporate social responsibility, and corporate governance.

A business ethics programme provides a toolkit of leadership and management practices to aid any enterprise-large or small-in the responsible pursuit of its envisioned future. It helps owners and managers ensure that their employees and agents comply with applicable laws and regulations. It also helps them minimise risk to the enterprise, enhance the enterprise's reputation, and bring value to stakeholders by adapting emerging global standards of responsible business conduct and best practices.

Medium-sized Enterprises

Small to medium-sized enterprises (SMEs) have an additional incentive to adopt the discipline of responsible business conduct: to create a wider commercial network. Where owners and managers embrace the global language of responsible business through a business ethics programme, a network of business enterprises and supportive NGOs based on shared values is possible. Such a network allows the individual SME to develop some of the synergies and economies of scale that only larger enterprises can afford.

Global Standards

Particularly over the past two decades, a number of prominent business associations, NGOs, and international government institutions have developed a body of global standards for the responsible business. These emerging global standards are of four types:

— A stakeholder engagement standard (AA1000S)

— Substantive standards (such as SA8000, Caux Round Table's principles, Interfaith Declaration's principles, and the Basic Guidelines for Codes of Business Conduct)

— Management process standards (such as SA8000, the CERES Principles, and the U.S. Federal Sentencing Guidelines for Organisations)

— Reporting standards (such as the Global Reporting Initiative)

The major standards-setting institutions are of three major types: business associations, stakeholder groups, and international governmental organisations.

Business associations that set standards include the following:

— *Caux Round Table*. A global network of business leaders committed to principled business leadership, the Caux Round Table believes that business has a crucial role in developing and promoting equitable solutions to key global issues. The Caux Round Table's Principles for Business serves as a guide to sustainable and socially responsible prosperity as the foundation for a fair, free, and transparent society.

International Chamber of Commerce (ICC)

— The International Chamber of Commerce (ICC) champions the global economy as a force for economic growth, job creation, and prosperity. ICC activities cover a broad spectrum, from performing arbitration and dispute resolution to making the case for open trade, the market economy system, and business selfregulation. The ICC's report, Extortion and Bribery in International Business Transactions, is another resource that helps fight corruption and commercial crime. The ICC has direct access to national governments and intergovernmental organisations on issues that directly affect business operations.

— Coalition for Environmentally Responsible Economies. A U.S. coalition of environmental, investor, and advocacy groups working together for a sustainable future, the Coalition for Environmentally Responsible Economies (CERES) is committed to continuous environmental improvement. It encourages enterprises to adopt the "CERES Principles," a 10-point code of environmental conduct.

— Institute of Electrical and Electronics Engineers. The Institute of Electrical and Electronics Engineers (IEEE) is a non-profit, technical professional association of more than 377,000 individual members in 150 countries. Its "Code of Ethics" contains 10 points of agreements to regulate the professional activities of its members. It also has a more detailed "Software Engineering Code of Ethics and Professional Practices" organised under eight principles. The IEEE has an ethics committee and an ethics hot-line.

Nongovernmental Organisations

Stakeholder groups such as the following also set standards:

— *Interfaith Declaration*. The Interfaith Declaration provides principles and guidelines to help practitioners identify the role they and their organisations should play in the community and to support problem solving. Particularly valuable are its "Principles for Global Corporate Responsibility: Benchmarks for Measuring Business Performance."

— *Global Reporting Initiative*. The Global Reporting Initiative (GRI) was established in late 1997 with the mission of developing globally applicable guidelines for reporting on economic, environmental, and social performance, initially for corporations and eventually for any business, government entity, or NGO. Convened by CERES in partnership with the United Nations Environment Programme, the GRI incorporates the active participation of corporations, NGOs, accounting organisations, business associations, and other stakeholders from around the world. The GRI's Sustainability Reporting Guidelines represent the first global framework for comprehensive sustainability reporting, encompassing the triple bottom line of financial, social, and environmental issues.

— *Social Accountability International*. A non-profit organisation, Social Accountability International (SAI) is dedicated to the development, implementation, and oversight of voluntary verifiable social accountability standards. SAI is committed to ensuring that standards and systems for verifying compliance with such standards are highly reputable and publicly accessible. SAI works to improve workplaces and combat sweatshops through the expansion and further development of the international workplace standard, SA8000, and the associated SA8000 verification system.

— *Global Sullivan Principles*. In 1977, the Rev. Leon H. Sullivan developed the "Sullivan Principles," a code of conduct for human rights and equal opportunity for companies operating in South Africa. To further expand human rights and economic development to all communities, Sullivan created the "Global Sullivan Principles of Social Responsibility" in 1997.

— *International Corporate Governance Network*. A membership association, the International Corporate Governance Network is devoted to improving corporate governance internationally and providing a voice between investors and management. As of 2001, its members owned or managed US$10 trillion.

— *Institute of Directors in Southern Africa*. In July 1993, the Institute of Directors in Southern Africa established the King Committee on Corporate Governance. The King Committee has produced two reports on corporate governance for Southern Africa.

— *Institute of Social and Ethical Account Ability*. In 1999, the Institute of Social and Ethical Accountability launched the AA1000 Framework. AA1000S is an accountability standard designed to help enterprises improve accountability and performance by learning through stakeholder engagement and by integrating their stakeholder engagement processes into daily activities. AA1000S helps users establish a systematic stakeholder engagement process that generates the indicators, targets, and reporting systems needed to ensure the effectiveness of the process in overall organisational performance. AA1000S is designed to complement the GRI's Sustainability Reporting Guidelines.

International Governmental Groups

International governmental groups also set standards as shown below::

— *International Labour Organisation*. The International Labour Organisation (ILO) is the U.N. agency that seeks to promote social justice and internationally recognised human and labour rights. The ILO formulates international labour standards in the form of conventions and recommendations setting minimum standards of basic labour rights: the freedom to associate, the right to organise, the right to collective bargaining, the abolition of forced labour, the right to equal opportunity and treatment, and other standards regulating conditions across the entire spectrum of work-related issues. Within the U.N. system, the ILO has a unique tripartite structure, with workers and employers participating as equal partners with governments in the work of its governing organs.

— *Organisation for Economic Cooperation and Development*. Thirty countries sharing a commitment to democratic government and the market economy form the Organisation for Economic Cooperation and Development (OECD). Having active relationships with some 70 other countries, NGOs, and civil society, the OECD has a global reach. It plays a prominent role in fostering good governance in the public service and in corporate activity.

— *U.N. Global Compact.* U.N. Secretary-General Kofi Annan first proposed the Global Compact in an address to the World Economic Forum on January 31, 1999. Annan challenged business leaders to join an international initiative-the Global Compact-that would bring companies together with U.N. agencies, labour, and civil society to support nine principles in the areas of human rights, labour, and the environment. Through the power of collective action, the Global Compact seeks to advance responsible corporate citizenship so that business can be part of the solution to the challenges of globalisation. In this way, the private sector-in partnership with other social actors-can help realise Annan's vision: a more sustainable and inclusive global economy.

— *U.S. Department of Commerce.* In cooperation with the Russian Chamber of Commerce and Industry, the U.S. Department of Commerce developed the Basic Guidelines for Codes of Business Conduct to reflect extensive input from Russian and U.S. trade organisations and businesses provided in the course of roundtables and discussions conducted in Russia and the United States.

References

Marcoux, A. (2009). *Business-Focused Business Ethics. Normative theory and Business Ethics*. J. Smith. New York, Rowman & Littlefield: 17–34.

Maxwell, J. C. (2003). *There is no such thing as business ethics*. New York, Warner Books.

Michelman, F. I. (1982). *Ethics, Economics, and the Law of Property. Nomos: Ethics, Economics, and the Law*. J. R. Pennock and J. W. Chapman. New York, New York University Press. 24: 3–40.

Moore, G. (2009). *Virtue Ethics and Business Organizations. Normative theory and business ethics*. J. Smith. New York, Rowman & Littlefield: 35–60.

13

Sustainable Business Environment

International business includes all business transactions that involve two or more countries. These transactions can be conducted exclusively in the private sector, or they can also involve the public sector. Companies get involved in international business for a variety of reasons. The major reason is to expand sales, perhaps because a firm has excess capacity and does not have additional sales opportunities at home. Thus, it needs to sell products abroad to utilise its capacity more efficiently. International sales can also be profitable.

A second reason to get involved in international business is to gain access to raw materials or other factors of production. Mining and agricultural companies operate in countries where natural resources or climate allow them to pursue their activities. On the other hand, manufacturing companies have found many developing countries in Eastern Europe, Asia, and Latin America to be ideal for doing business because of cheap labour and overhead-type expenses. Thus, they have expanded abroad to gain production efficiencies.

A third incentive for international activity is to gain access to knowledge. Learning about new technology quickly can make a big difference in a company's ability to compete in global markets. New technology is being developed worldwide, so companies cannot rely on their domestic market to keep abreast of new developments.

When companies, and especially the market seekers, first begin to expand beyond domestic markets, they usually get involved in exports and imports. Merchandise exports are goods sent out of a country, and merchandise imports are goods brought into a country. Exports and imports can also involve services as well as goods. Service exports refer to the receipt of earnings from the performance of services abroad. For example, if KPMG sent auditors to different countries to perform an audit and received a fee for those services, that work would be considered a service export. The country where the work was performed would experience a service import, which would result in an outflow of cash to the exporting country. Other examples of services are travel, tourism, and transportation.

In addition to exporting and importing, companies can expand abroad through one of several types of strategic alliances. A strategic alliance is used to describe a wide variety of collaborations, which are of strategic importance to one or more of the parties involved. Strategic alliances include licensing agreements, franchising, management contracts, custom contracts, and shared ownership of foreign companies. The choice of the type of strategic alliance depends on legal factors, cost, experience, competition, risk, control, and product complexity. Two similar strategic alliances involve a licensing agreement and a franchise agreement. A licensing agreement exists when one company grants rights to intangible property to another company for a specified period of time in return for a royalty.

The intangible property might involve a production process, formula, design, pattern, patent, or invention. Companies enter into licensing agreements to earn a return on their intellectual property without having to undertake the risk of expanding abroad using their own capital. A franchise, such as those of Holiday Inn or McDonald's, involves the use of a trademark that is an essential asset but also provision of assistance on a continual basis in running the business. Holiday Inn, for example, provides a reservation service for franchisees and continual audits on quality, and so on. Sometimes companies will cooperate in the development of new technology or in producing goods and services.

Companies can also invest abroad. A direct investment occurs when a company assumes some degree of control over a foreign corporation in order to influence management decisions. The decision can occur in the form of an acquisition of existing stock in a local firm or in the establishment of a "greenfield investment," which is the establishment of a new firm in a foreign location. If the investor owns

100 percent of the stock in the local firm, that firm becomes a wholly owned subsidiary. If two or more firms are involved in establishing a venture, the operation is known as a joint venture, another form of strategic alliance. Joint ventures often occur because the investor lacks financial or managerial expertise or because the investor needs to rely on the local knowledge of the partner in the venture.

MULTINATIONAL ENTERPRISES (MNE)

A variety of terms describe companies involved in international business. The most frequently used term is multinational enterprise (MNE), which refers to companies that have a worldwide view of production, the sourcing of raw materials and components, and final markets. There is no consensus as to how much of a company's sales, assets, earnings, and employees must be abroad for the firm to be considered an MNE, but anything less than 10 percent of these indicators would probably disqualify a company from the elite group of MNEs. More than 10 percent implies that the companies are operating in at least two countries, and most MNEs have significant geographical spread.

The lack of a global vision is another indicator that a company is not yet an MNE. Another indicator of multinational involvement is the degree of international experience of key executives. MNEs adopt different strategies to operate internationally, including transnational, global, and multidomestic strategies. The term MNE to refer to companies that are operating in many different countries, regardless of the specific strategic approach they use to sell products and source production.

It is difficult to identify precisely the largest MNEs in the world because there are different definitions of size. The two most commonly used measures for size are market value and sales. In addition, other measures, such as profits and return on shareholders' equity, are often used to compare companies worldwide.

Japan has the second largest number of companies with 137, and Britain is third with 73 companies. There are companies from seven developing countries, primarily from Asia and Latin America, with India having the largest number of companies at 8, closely followed by China and Mexico with 6 companies each. It is interesting to note that

Wal-Mart de Mexico is the third largest company in Mexico, while its parent, Wal-Mart Stores of the United States is the fifth largest company in the world in market value and #1 in sales. Gazprom of Russia is the 47th largest company in the world in market value, the highest-ranking company from a developing country.

Most of the companies in the top 50 would also qualify as MNEs because of the importance of global markets to sales. It is interesting to note that the firms on the list are from a variety of industries. Even though the large MNEs are the ones most noticed and discussed, a company does not have to be large to be engaged in international business. The probability that a firm will engage in international transactions increases with firm size and as the firm begins to saturate the domestic environment. However, even small companies can export or import, manufacture products abroad or source production to independent manufacturers abroad, or get involved in licensing agreements. This is especially true of high-tech start-up companies that often get involved in international business immediately. In addition, some companies such as Nike design products in the domestic market but

Decision to Become Global

The decision to become global depends on how effectively management assesses two different but interactive dimensions: the external environment and the internal capabilities of the firm.

Environmental constraints strongly influence the elements of the management process, which in turn affect management and managerial effectiveness, which determines firm efficiency. The environmental constraints are grouped into four categories: educational, sociological (or sociocultural), political and legal, and economic. The educational characteristics include the level of literacy, the availability of specialised and higher education, the attitude toward education, and the match of education with skill requirements in the economy. Sociocultural characteristics include the attitude toward managers and authority, interorganisational cooperation, attitude toward achievement and work, class structure and individual mobility, and attitudes toward wealth, rationality, risk taking, and change.

Among the major political and legal characteristics are the relevant legal rules of the game and flexibility in their application, defense and foreign policy, political stability, and political organisation. Key economic characteristics are the general economic framework, fiscal and monetary policy, economic stability, capital markets, factor endowments, and market size.

Environmental constraints can rarely be changed by the MNE, so management has to decide whether or not those constraints would permit successful foreign investment. Sometimes management becomes overwhelmed with the differences and takes a polycentric attitude, which implies that all operating policies and procedures must be adjusted to the local environment. This is especially true of MNEs from the Western Hemisphere investing in Asia. In other cases, management takes an ethnocentric attitude, which means that everything the MNE does in the home country can be transferred to the foreign country, in spite of the environmental differences. Although the MNE can act as an agent of change in many circumstances, the ethnocentric attitude is usually a little extreme.

An important dimension of the environmental constraints is that some countries might have country-specific advantages, also known as location-specific advantages, that might strongly influence foreign investment. For example, the existence of a key natural resource; the availability of a plentiful, cheap labour supply; or the presence of a large market are country-specific advantages and are reasons why an MNE might want to invest in a particular location. These country-specific advantages would exist as incentives, rather than barriers, to investment.

The firmspecific advantages, also called ownership-specific advantages, relate primarily to the intangible assets that the firm possesses. In many cases, MNEs are basically in oligopolistic industries. However, smaller firms may have a firmspecific advantage because of a market niche or unique product capability. Typically, these firmspecific advantages are not easily duplicated by competitors, except in the long run or at very high costs. Thus, "The core skill of the MNE can be some element of its management structure, marketing techniques, or overall strategic planning that leads to a firmspecific advantage.

These firmspecific advantages are modelled as endogenous to the MNEs, since their internal markets permit the MNEs to control them". A firm with a set of firmspecific advantages has a variety of options available for their productive use. The firm could exploit this advantage through exports. However, barriers to exports then lead the firm to explore other options. Selling the firmspecific advantage to another firm is a possibility, but the gains from the sale would not be as high as they would if the firm were to use the firmspecific advantage internally. A firm that decides to use the firmspecific advantages rather than sell them to other firms internalizes the firmspecific advantages.

Orgins of Accounting and International Business

Now that we have examined the origins of accounting and international business, let's focus more specifically on factors in the domestic and international environment that influence accounting. To a large extent, corporate accounting and information disclosure practices are influenced by a variety of economic, social, and political factors. A model of the environmental influences is presented in Figure 1. These include the nature of enterprise ownership, the business activities of the enterprise, sources of finance and the stage of development of capital markets, the nature of the taxation system, the existence and significance of the accounting profession, the state of accounting education and research, the nature of the political system, the social climate, the stage of economic growth and development, the rate of inflation, the nature of the legal system, and the nature of accounting regulation. The nature of accounting systems at the country level will vary according to the relative influence of these environmental factors; such systems will, in turn, tend to reinforce established patterns of behaviour.

With respect to enterprise ownership, the need for public accountability and disclosure will be greater where there is a broad ownership of shares compared to family ownership. Where there is state ownership, the influence of centralised control on accounting systems will tend to override the serving of microeconomic objectives. The activities of enterprises will also influence the nature of the accounting system depending on whether the business is agricultural, extractive, or manufacturing; whether it is diversified; whether it is multinational; and whether it is a large group of companies or a small business.

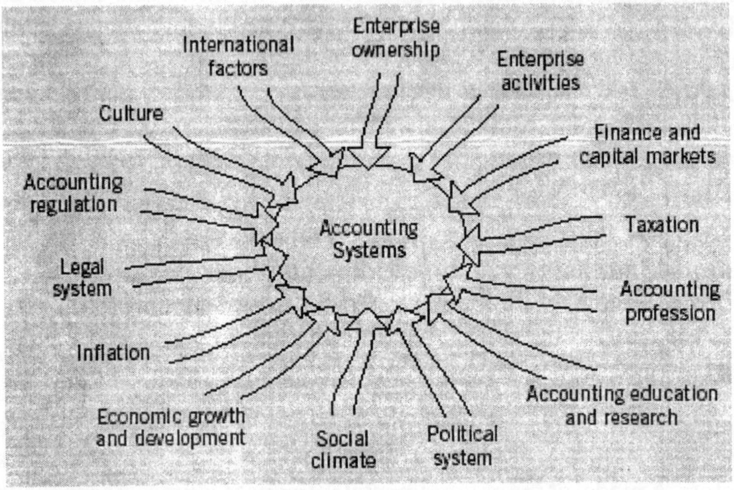

Figure 1. Environmental Influences on accounting development

The sources of finance are another important influence. Clearly, there will be more pressure for public accountability and information disclosure when finance is raised from external shareholders via stock exchanges rather than banks or family sources, where information will be available more directly. Taxation is a very important factor in situations where accounting systems are strongly influenced by state objectives; that is, in countries like France and Germany, public accounting reports are used as a basis for determining tax liabilities. In the United States and the United Kingdom, on the other hand, the published accounts are adjusted for tax purposes and submitted separately from the reports to shareholders.

Where there is a more developed accounting profession there are likely to be more developed, judgmentally based public accounting systems rather than more centralised and uniform systems. Furthermore, the development of professional accounting will depend on the existence of a sound infrastructure of accounting education and research, which is often lacking in developing countries. The political system is obviously a very important influence on accounting in that the nature of the accounting system will reflect political philosophies and objectives (e.g., central planning versus private enterprise). The social climate, that is, attitudes toward informing and consulting employees and toward environmental concerns, will also be influential. In Europe, for example, there is a much more positive approach to the disclosure of information relating to such matters than in the United States.

The nature and extent of economic growth and development will also be influential insofar as a change from an agricultural to a manufacturing economy will pose new accounting problems, such as the depreciation of machinery, leasing, and so on. In many countries, services are now becoming more important, and thus problems related to how to account for intangible assets such as brand names, goodwill, and human resources have become significant. Inflation is often associated with economic growth and is a major influence on accounting where hyperinflation has been rife (e.g., in South America) to the extent that alternative systems to the traditional historical cost approach are often used.

The legal system is also important in determining the extent to which company law governs the regulation of accounting. In countries such as France and Germany, with a tradition of codified Roman law (or civil codes)-versus common law as in the United Kingdom and the United States-accounting regulations tend to be detailed and comprehensive. Furthermore, the accounting profession tends to have much less influence in setting accounting standards in such countries compared to countries such as the United Kingdom and the United States, where company law is supplemented by professional regulation.

In addition, the influence of culture (i.e., societal or national values) on accounting traditions and practices needs to be taken into account. International factors are also bringing about changes in the environment that are creating harmonisation in international accounting in contrast to the constraining influences operating at national levels. One important international factor is colonial influence. Countries that are former colonies of the United Kingdom tend to use the British approach to accounting, whereas former French colonies tend to use the French system.

In addition, membership in regional trade blocs, such as the European Union, often results in a convergence of accounting standards for countries within the bloc. Finally, the International Accounting Standards Board, an international organisation dedicated to the convergence of accounting standards worldwide, is working hard to bridge the differences in accounting standards worldwide so that investors can make decisions based on common accounting standards and practices worldwide. Naturally, the influence of these factors is dynamic and will vary both between and within countries over time.

Moreover, an evolutionary process of some complexity appears to be at work that is reflected in a growing number of international and regional influences. These include the activities of MNEs and intergovernmental organisations such as the United Nations (UN), the Organisation of Economic Cooperation and Development (OECD), and the European Union. In the European context, the European Union is an especially significant influence in that any agreement on the harmonisation of accounting and information disclosure eventually becomes legally enforceable through a process of implementation in the national laws of the member countries.

Although there are many differences in national environments, with correspondingly varying effects on accounting systems, there are also many similarities. Attempts to classify countries and identify patterns or groupings are still very much in the early stages. However, such efforts appear to be a useful way to gain a better understanding of the key factors influencing the development of accounting systems and thus help us predict likely changes and their impact.

Accounting systems in socialist economies tend to be quite different from those in developed market economies such as the United States, Japan, and the EU countries. In the former socialist economies of Russia and Eastern Europe, for example, accounting is making a transition to a market approach. As far as public accounting and reporting in the market economies are concerned, however, a number of distinct models of accounting appear to be identifiable, including, at the very least, the British-American and continental European traditions.

But given the factors of change at work, making accurate assessments or predictions about the future evolution of accounting is difficult. Because of the activities of many national and international organisations and the changing nature of business and especially multinational operations, accounting today is in a state of flux. It may well be that new models or patterns of accounting and reporting are being formed. The British and continental European traditions, for example, are now being coordinated and to some extent fused through EU efforts to harmonise accounting.

New Trends in Markets Securities

There has been a strong move among securities markets to attract companies from abroad to list on their exchanges. In 2004, for example, the trading volume of non- U.S. firms listed on the New York Stock Exchange was 10.5 percent of the Exchange's total trading volume. Although that is a relatively small percentage, that trading volume on its own would make trading in non-U.S. listed companies the second largest market in the world. However, the new Sarbanes-Oxley law on corporate governance and internal controls must be applied to foreign listers on any U.S. exchange, and the law is proving to be a barrier to attracting new business and even holding on to existing business.

Another trend in securities trading in Europe has to do with the consolidation of European stock exchanges. Prior to the 1999 introduction of the euro, the common currency used in Europe, there were 32 different stock exchanges in Europe. Three stock exchanges dominate trading in Europe-the Frankfurt Stock Exchange, the London Stock Exchange, and Euronext NV, which includes the French, Dutch, Belgian, and Portuguese stock and futures markets and the London International Financial Futures & Options Exchange, known as Life.

Consolidation of other exchanges has taken place as well, such as the creation of Eurex, the joining together of the German and Swiss futures and options exchanges, which created the world's biggest derivatives exchange. The Finnish and Swedish exchanges also combined into one exchange called OMX AB. The move to consolidate derives from the increase in competition to offer the lowest fees for listing and trading securities.

Markets in developing countries are growing as well. One reason is the overall growth in business and the desire of companies to access capital markets instead of relying on banks and family wealth. Another reason is the privatisation of national companies as countries try to reduce budget deficits and get their economies under control. Also lurking on the horizon is China, which is opening up its borders to foreign direct investments and is increasingly changing its business model to that of a market economy. Even though the overall market capitalisation of the developing countries is relatively small compared to that of the industrial countries, it is clearly increasing.

A Wider Audience

Accountability and information disclosure by corporations has developed historically in response to those with direct financial investment. In recent years, however, there has been an increasing acknowledgment that since finance providers, such as shareholders, bankers, lenders, and creditors, are not the only group affected by the actions of a corporation, there is an obligation to report to a wider audience, which includes employees, trade unions, consumers, government agencies, and the general public. There are a variety of reasons for this widespread belief that companies should explicitly disclose information to groups other than finance providers.

One of the most significant reasons is the development and growth of the influence of trade unions and employees in most developed countries. They have been instrumental in voicing the view that those who are significantly affected by decisions made by institutions in general must be given the opportunity to influence those decisions. Furthermore, there is growing public concern about the impact of corporations on externalities (e.g., pollution of the environment and the influence of large corporations on national economic and social policies).

These developments, among others, have expanded the concept of "accountability" and the desire of various groups in society to monitor and influence the behaviour of business corporations. Wider corporate accountability thus has become an issue of major interest in recent years. To what extent has it affected corporate reports? The development of accounting by corporations has been constrained by restrictions on both the supply and demand sides.

On the supply side, explicit acknowledgment of the "rights" of nonfinance providers, such as trade unions, to information may, for some corporations, mean that they would be committed to pursue goals other than those they have traditionally followed. From a managerial perspective, this could endanger the growth or survival of the corporation. The extent to which corporations' behaviour has been influenced in the goals of nonfinance providers is another matter. But many corporations, regardless of what they actually do, have been reluctant to formally acknowledge the influence of other "stakeholders."

Corporate reports may be used as a source of information helpful for making decisions and reporting on management's stewardship to finance providers. Increasing information disclosure to nonfinance providers may be seen as increasing the power of the recipients to influence the behaviour of the corporation as well as providing material for criticism of the corporation's performance. A further constraint is that many of the expectations of nonfinance providers are not clearly defined, and the techniques to measure them do not exist. Although the information requests of finance providers relate to the periodic financial resources and position of a corporation and the results of its operations, many of the information requirements of nonfinance providers appear to relate to a corporation's social as well as economic performance.

Not only are measurement techniques often unavailable or underdeveloped but often there is not even general agreement on the broad elements of accountability involved. On the demand side, information already made available to the public may satisfy the demands of the nonfinance providers, making additional information unnecessary. The disclosure of additional information may not be that helpful. The ability of nonfinance providers to influence corporate behaviour varies considerably. Those with limited or no influence can exert little direct pressure for increased disclosure, whereas those with some power may be able to bypass the published corporate report and obtain information directly, and in greater detail, in special reports.

In many European countries, especially Germany and France, trade unions or employee representatives have, through various forms of "codetermination" or collective bargaining, obtained access to information. In Germany, for example, this right to disclosure is established in law, with works councils given access to a wide range of financial and nonfinancial information. The philosophy behind this is that such access will promote mutual trust between employers and employees. The availability of information for bargaining with corporations can be double-edged, however, in the sense that the information may not substantiate opinions previously held and could therefore reduce rather than enhance the influence of the user group concerned.

Foreign direct investment (FDI) by MNEs entails certain benefits and costs for host countries. In this context, the demand for greater disclosure from MNEs may be viewed as part of a bargaining process-an effort by host countries, and developing countries in particular, to improve their bargaining powers. The fact that MNEs operate in a number of different nation-states has given them an opportunity to take actions in their own best interest that are not available to others. This is the basis for a conflict of perspectives between that of a national view of various groups within the nation-state and the multinational view of the MNEs. While business activities in a single country are for many MNEs just a part of their global operation, this is the part that is of primary concern for most of those affected in the host country.

The multinationality, size, and complexity of MNEs have enabled some of them to undertake actions detrimental to a host country. Cases of tax avoidance bordering on evasion, political interference, discriminatory practices, and so on are well documented. Whether these are exceptions or whether they represent more general practice is a matter of debate. The known cases, however, have been sufficient when combined with other factors to increase the pressure for greater accountability and disclosure.

Accountability by MNEs thus may be differentiated from accountability by domestic corporations, though both are business organisations with many features in common. A domestic corporation's primary operations are in one country, and its cross-frontier relationships are with unrelated parties. On the other hand, MNEs operate in a number of countries with different laws and currencies, and there is usually a significant volume of transactions between units located in different countries. The common control of these globally dispersed operations provides the opportunity to coordinate pricing, sourcing, and location decisions in a manner that, while increasing the net return of the group, may be detrimental or, alternatively, advantageous to individual nation-states. This special impact of MNEs appears to have given rise to pressure for more accountability and information disclosure.

A firm's first exposure to international accounting usually occurs as a result of an import or export opportunity. In the case of exports, a domestic company may receive an unsolicited inquiry or purchase order from a foreign buyer. Assuming the domestic company desires to make the sale, it needs to investigate the foreign buyer, particularly when the buyer asks for the extension of credit. This procedure is often not as easy as it appears.

First, the buyer may not be listed in any of the international credit rating directories, such as Standard & Poor's. If not, the seller may need to ask its bank to have its foreign affiliates check on the buyer's creditability. Alternatively, it may ask the buyer to supply financial information. The buyer may be willing to supply financial statements, but these statements may be difficult for the domestic company to interpret. The statements may be in a foreign language and may be based on accounting assumptions and procedures unfamiliar to the company's accountants. Most companies new to international business must then get help, either from a bank or from an accounting firm with international expertise.

If the foreign buyer pays in its own currency, the selling company must become familiar with the potential gains and losses from changes in the exchange rate that may occur between the time the order is booked and the time the payment is received. The selling company must also deal with a host of other international details-special international shipping and insurance documents, customs declaration forms, international legal documents, and so on. Once again, the services of lawyers, shippers, bankers, and accountants with international expertise are needed.

In the case of a potential import, the international accounting aspects are not as involved because most of the details are the responsibility of the foreign seller. However, if the foreign seller requires payments in his or her currency or if the domestic buyer wants information about the reliability of the foreign supplier, the buyer may need to consult an international bank, lawyer, or accounting firm.

As the firm becomes increasingly involved in trade, the international accounting activity increases, and so do the costs of using outside expertise. At some point it becomes feasible for the company to develop the international capabilities of its own staff, including its own accountants. The next major development that is likely to necessitate increased international accounting skills is the creation of a separate organisation within the company to handle international trade. This may be an export department. Special accounting systems and procedures must be established in control, reporting, and taxation areas. Typically, the next evolutionary step is the establishment of a foreign operation of some kind. In the minimal case, the company may decide to license a foreign manufacturer to produce its product or some part of its product. This involves selecting a potential licensee, analysing its reliability and capability, and drawing up a contract. It also involves developing an accounting system to monitor contract performance and royalty and technical payments and to handle the foreign money flows into the company's tax and financial statements.

At the other end of the spectrum, the company may establish a wholly owned subsidiary in a foreign country. Accounting for the foreign subsidiary would include (1) meeting the requirements of the foreign government, which would be based on procedures and practices different from those in the parent company's country; (2) establishing a management information system to monitor, control, and evaluate the foreign subsidiary; and (3) developing a system to consolidate the foreign subsidiary's operating results with those of the parent for financial and taxreporting purposes.

Between these extremes are a host of alternatives: opening up a sales office, setting up a warehouse, forming a joint venture with another company, and buying into an existing company. Each brings with it new international dimensions and requirements for management and, more specifically, for the company's accountants. It should also be pointed out that, before any of this takes place, a thorough study of market conditions-legal, economic, political, and sociocultural-should be made, including detailed feasibility studies and risk analysis. All of these steps require the collection and appropriate analysis of information in both quantitative financial terms and qualitative terms.

During a first venture into any of these more advanced areas, the international expertise of outside groups can be indispensable because of the money and risks involved in international trade. However, using outside international experts in no way lessens the need to develop in-house international capabilities, not only in accounting but in other functional areas as well. Finally, some knowledge of international accounting may be necessary even if a firm is not involved in international business per se-for example, if the firm wishes to borrow money or to buy or sell stocks or bonds outside its home country. In some cases, it may be cheaper to borrow money or issue stocks or bonds abroad because interest rates are lower or exchange rate movements are favourable. In order to take advantage of these situations, the firm needs to know not only the relevant foreign laws, regulations, and customs but also the domestic legal, tax, and accounting treatments of any of these transactions.

Sustainable Business Development

Protecting an organisation's capital base is a well-accepted business principle. Yet organisations do not generally recognise the possibility of extending this notion to the world's natural and human resources. If sustainable development is to achieve its potential, it must be integrated into the planning and measurement systems of business enterprises. And for that to happen, the concept must be articulated in terms that are familiar to business leaders.

The World Commission on Environment and Development, recognises that economic development must meet the needs of a business enterprise and its stakeholders. The latter include shareholders, lenders, customers, employees, suppliers and communities who are affected by the organisation's activities. It also highlights business's dependence on human and natural resources, in addition to physical and financial capital. It emphasizes that economic activity must not irreparably degrade or destroy these natural and human resources.

Sustainable development is a pervasive philosophy to which every participant in the global economy (including consumers and government) must subscribe, if we are to meet today's needs without compromising the ability of future generations to meet their own.

IMPLICATIONS

It has become a cliché that environmental problems are substantial, and that economic growth contributes to them. A common response is stricter environmental regulation, which often inhibits growth. The result can be a trade-off between a healthy environment on the one hand and healthy growth on the other. As a consequence, opportunities for business may be constrained.

However, there are some forms of development that are both environmentally and socially sustainable. They lead not to a trade-off but to an improved environment, together with development that does not draw down our environmental capital. This is what sustainable development is all about—a revolutionary change in the way we approach these issues.

Businesses and societies can find approaches that will move towards all three goals—environmental protection, social wellbeing and economic development—at the same time. Sustainable development is good business in itself. It creates opportunities for suppliers of 'green consumers', developers of environmentally safer materials and processes, firms that invest in eco-efficiency, and those that engage themselves in social well-being. These enterprises will generally have a competitive advantage. They will earn their local community's goodwill and see their efforts reflected in the bottom line.

While business traditionally seeks precision and practicality as the basis for its planning efforts, sustainable development is a concept that is not amenable to simple and universal definition. It is fluid, and changes over time in response to increased information and society's evolving priorities.

The role of business in contributing to sustainable development remains indefinite. While all business enterprises can make a contribution towards its attainment, the ability to make a difference varies by sector and organisation size. Some executives consider the principal objective of business to be making money. Others recognise a broader social role. There is no consensus among business leaders as to the best balance between narrow self-interest and actions taken for the good of society. Companies continually face the need to trade off what they would 'like' to do and what they 'must' do in pursuit of financial survival.

Businesses also face trade-offs when dealing with the transition to sustainable practices. For example, a chemical company whose plant has excessive effluent discharges might decide to replace it with a more effective treatment facility. But should the company close the existing plant during the two or three-year construction period and risk losing market share? Or should it continue to operate the polluting plant despite the cost of fines and adverse public relations? Which is the better course of action in terms of economy, social wellbeing and the environment?

Moreover, many areas of sustainable development remain technically ambiguous, making it difficult to plan an effective course of action. For example, the forestry industry has had difficulty defining what constitutes sustainable forest management. Some critics believe that simply replacing trees is not enough, because harvesting destroys the biodiversity of the forest. Clearly, more research will be needed to resolve such technical issues.

From a broader perspective, however, it is clearly in the interest of business to operate within a healthy environment and economy. It is equally plain that, on a global basis, growing and sustainable economies in the developing countries will provide the best opportunities for expanding markets. To some, sustainable development and environmental stewardship are synonymous. In the short term, sound environmental performance is probably a reasonable objective for most businesses, with sustainable development as a longer term goal. However, this can lead to confusion. In the developed world, the focus is on environmental management, while in developing countries, rapid and sustainable development is paramount.

The global economy is coming under growing pressure to pay for the restoration of damaged environments. But this economic engine is being asked to help solve other pressing problems at the same time. The challenge is to solve all of these problems in a sustainable manner, so as to generate continuing development. Despite ambiguities about definitions, there is now widespread support for sustainable development principles within the business community. However, for that support to grow, it will be important to recognise and reward initiatives that are being taken to turn the concept into reality.

Changes

William Mulligan, environmental affairs manager at Chevron Corporation, reflects the view of many in the business community who believe that the environment is now a major issue - one which presents both challenges and opportunities. 'Over the last decade, we have seen many polls confirming the importance of the environment to Americans,' he says. 'Only an irresponsible company would dismiss this trend as a passing fad or fail to recognise the need to integrate environmental considerations into every aspect of its business. Environmental excellence has to become part of strategic thinking. It is in our best economic interests to do so. In fact, whenever we are forced to change, we often find opportunities.'

This positive change in attitudes and practices is echoed by the Organisation for Economic Cooperation and Development, which says: 'There is now a realistic prospect of harmonising environmental and economic considerations, and thus of gradually incorporating these objectives in policy.'

Many executives have demonstrated that pursuing sustainable development strategies makes good business sense. For example, a 3M manufacturing plant scaled down a wastewater treatment operation by half, simply by running cooling water through its factories repeatedly instead of discharging it after a single use. Meanwhile Dow's 'Waste Reduction Always Pays' programme, which began in 1986, has fostered more than 700 projects, and saved millions of dollars a year. And in a Westinghouse metal finishing factory in Puerto Rico, the company reduced 'dragout' - the contamination accidentally carried from one tank to another - by 75% simply by shaking the tank to remove solids before releasing the chemical to the next tank.

Pacific Gas and Electric decided that energy conservation was a more profitable investment than nuclear power, and Mc Donald's made its well-publicised move from plastics to paper the cornerstone of a much broader, but less visible, waste reduction strategy. The managers of these businesses clearly believe that environmentalism has something to offer business. In an interview with Tomorrow magazine, John Elkington of environmental consultancy Sustainability says: 'We are seeing the birth of corporate environmentalism. In fact the main impetus for sustainable development in the future will probably come from business.'

There are other significant developments too, Elkington points out. Many consumers are now prepared to pay more for environmentally responsible products. And the emergence of ethical investment funds has thrown the spotlight onto corporate environmental performance. Also significant, says Elkington, is that companies are changing from within, rather than simply responding to external pressure from consumers and environmentalists.

Sustainable Development Principles

The concept of sustainable development needs to be incorporated into the policies and processes of a business if it is to follow sustainable development principles. This does not mean that new management methods need to be invented. Rather, it requires a new cultural orientation and extensive refinements to systems, practices and procedures. The two main areas of the management system that must be changed are those concerned with:

— A greater accountability to non-traditional stakeholders;

— Continuous improvement of reporting practices.

Developing an effective management framework for sustainable development requires addressing both decisionmaking and governance. The concept of sustainable development must be integrated both into business planning and into management information and control systems. Senior management must provide reports that measure performance against these strategies.

Governance is increasingly important because of the growing accountability of the corporation and its senior management. Information and reporting systems must support this need. Decisionmaking at all levels must become more responsive to the issues arising from sustainable development. Seven steps are required for managing an enterprise according to sustainable development principles. These are set out below.

A stakeholder analysis is required in order to identify all the parties that are directly or indirectly affected by the enterprise's operations. It sets out the issues, concerns and information needs of the stakeholders with respect to the organisation's sustainable development activities. A company's existence is directly linked to the global environment as well as to the community in which it is based. In carrying out its activities, a company must maintain respect for human dignity, and strive towards a society where the global environment is protected.

At the beginning of this century, company strategies were directed primarily towards earning the maximum return for shareholders and investors. Businesses were not expected to achieve any other social or environmental objectives. Exploitation of natural and human resources was the norm in many industries, as was a lack of regard for the wellbeing of the communities in which the enterprise operated. In short, corporations were accountable only to their owners.

Today, business enterprises in developed countries operate in a more complicated, and more regulated, environment. Numerous laws and regulations govern their activities, and make their directors accountable to a broader range of stakeholders. Sustainable development extends the stakeholder group even further, by including future generations and natural resources. Identifying the parties that have a vested interest in a business enterprise is a central component of the sustainable development concept, and leads to greater corporate accountability. Developing a meaningful approach to stakeholder analysis is a vital aspect of this management system, and one of the key differences between sustainable and conventional management practices.

The stakeholder analysis begins by identifying the various groups affected by the business's activities. These include shareholders, creditors, regulators, employees, customers, suppliers, and the community in which the enterprise operates. It must also include people who are affected, or who consider themselves affected, by the enterprise's effect on the biosphere and on social capital. This is not a case of altruism on the company's part, but rather good business.

Companies that understand what their stakeholders want will be able to capitalise on the opportunities presented. They will benefit from a better informed and more active workforce, and better information in the capital markets. In identifying stakeholder groups, management should consider every business activity and operating location. Some stakeholders, such as shareholders, may be common to all activities or locations. Others, such as local communities, will vary according to business location and activity. Finally, the stakeholder analysis needs to consider the effect of the business's activities on the environment, the public at large, and the needs of future generations.

After the stakeholders have been identified, management should prepare a description of the needs and expectations that these groups have. This should set out both current and future needs, in order to capture sustainable development concept. The key is to analyse how the organisation's activities affect each set of stakeholders, either positively or negatively. Developing these statements of needs and expectations requires dialogue with each stakeholder group. To this end, some companies have established community advisory panels. Similar groups made up of employees, shareholders and suppliers have been used to help management better understand their needs and expectations. Because the needs of stakeholder groups are constantly evolving, monitoring them is an ongoing process.

The stakeholder analysis may reveal conflicting expectations. For example, customers may demand new, environmentally safe products, while employees might be concerned that such a policy could threaten their jobs. Shareholders, meanwhile, may be wary about the return on their investment. A stakeholder analysis can be a useful way to identify areas of potential conflict among stakeholder groups before they materialise.

The next objective is to articulate the basic values that the enterprise expects its employees to follow with respect to sustainable development, and to set targets for operating performance. Senior management is responsible for formulating a sustainable development policy for its organisation, and for establishing specific objectives. Sustainable development means more than just 'the environment'. It has social elements as well, such as the alleviation of poverty and distributional equity.

It also takes into account economic considerations that may be absent from a strictly 'environmental' viewpoint. In particular, it emphasizes maintaining or enhancing the world's capital endowment, and highlights limits to society's ability to substitute manmade capital for natural capital. Nevertheless, a policy on environmental responsibility is a good first step towards the broader concerns of sustainable development.

Management should incorporate stakeholder expectations into a broad policy statement that sets out the organisation's mission with respect to sustainable development. This policy statement would guide the planning process and put forward values towards which management, employees and other groups such as suppliers are expected to strive. Drafting a policy statement that is both inspirational and capable of influencing behaviour is a challenging task. However, the benefits justify the effort.

The following policy statement was developed by the Dow Chemical Company:

> The operating units of the Dow Chemical Company are committed to continued excellence, leadership and stewardship in protecting and conserving the environment for future generations. This is a primary management responsibility as well as the responsibility of every employee worldwide. We are sensitive to the concerns of the public and accountable to them for our decisions and actions. We believe in the responsible integration of environmental and economic considerations in all decisions affecting our operations. We are continuously reducing our emissions to protect human health and the environment. Our goal is the elimination of wastes and emissions.

Policy statements like this one should be developed and implemented in a way that visibly involves directors and senior management. A survey by DRT International of European companies found that half of the respondents have board members who are responsible for environmental issues. The report adds:

> The amount of time spent on environmental issues at board level varies greatly between countries and sectors. The greatest involvement is found in the chemical and pharmaceutical industries and in utilities. These sectors devote significant resources to planning green strategies and establishing sophisticated environmental management systems. The lowest involvement is in tourism and financial services, where none of the companies surveyed had board-level appointments.

There are many benefits in actively involving the board of directors in the development of a sustainable development policy. It is the board of directors that determines overall priorities and sets the tone for management and employees. By itself, the board's commitment will not guarantee that a sustainable development policy will be effectively implemented. However, the absence of that commitment will certainly make it difficult to implement the policy.

While statements of broad policy on sustainable development are important, senior management and directors should supplement their policy statement with a series of specific objectives. For example, the following statement of policy and objectives, developed by Northern Telecom, illustrates the desirable scope and level of specificity:

> Recognising the critical link between a healthy environment and sustained economic growth, we are committed to leading the telecommunications industry in protecting and enhancing the environment. Such stewardship is indispensable to our continued business success. Therefore, wherever we do business, we will take the initiative in developing innovative solutions to those environmental issues that affect our business.

We will:

— Integrate environmental considerations into our business planning and decisionmaking processes, including product research and development, new manufacturing methods and acquisitions/divestitures;

— Identify, assess and manage environmental risks associated with our operations and products throughout their life cycle, to reduce or eliminate the likelihood of adverse consequences;

— Comply with all applicable legal and regulatory requirements and, to the extent we determine it appropriate, adopt more stringent standards for the protection of our employees and the communities in which we operate;

— Establish a formal Environmental Protection Programme, and set specific, measurable goals;

— Establish assurance programmes, including regular audits, to assess the success of the Environmental Protection Programme in meeting regulatory requirements, programme goals and good practices;

— To the extent that proven technology will allow, eliminate or reduce harmful discharges, hazardous materials and waste;

— Make reduction, reuse and recycling the guiding principles and means by which we achieve our goals;

— Prepare and make public an annual report summarising our environmental activities;

— Work as advocates with our suppliers, customers and business partners to jointly achieve the highest possible environmental standards;

— Build relationships with other environmental stakeholders - including governments, the scientific community, educational institutions, public interest groups and the general public - to promote the development and communication of innovative solutions to industry environmental problems;

— Provide regular communications to, and training for, employees to heighten awareness of, and pride in, environmental issues.

It is important that sustainable development objectives be clear, concise and, wherever possible, expressed in measurable terms. Establishing measurable objectives is essential if management and others are to be able to assess whether their business activities have met the established objectives.

In setting these objectives, management will need to determine the appropriate level of aggregation. For example, one objective might be to set measurable performance targets for waste reduction at all operating locations. This goal would then be supported by more detailed objectives for each operating location.

After the sustainable development objectives have been established, management should compare its competitive and financial strategies against these targets. In some areas, business strategies will be consistent with the sustainable development objectives. In others, existing strategies may be incomplete or in conflict with them. Consequently, strategies may have to be modified.

It is important to ensure that the sustainable development objectives that are established complement the enterprise's existing competitive strategies. In other words, sustainable development should provide an additional dimension to business strategy. It provides senior management with an additional benchmark against which business strategies and performance should be assessed.

An effective external monitoring system is necessary for directors and senior management, in order to ensure that sustainable development policies, objectives and management systems are appropriate for the complex and rapidly changing world in which their business operates. Information should be gathered on key subjects, including:

— New and proposed legislation;
— Industry practices and standards;
— Competitors' strategies;
— Community and special interest group policies and activities;
— Trade union concerns;
— Technical developments, such as new process technologies.

For many enterprises, monitoring and influencing external developments means becoming more actively involved in the public policy process. A commitment to sustainable development involves helping to formulate policies that shape external developments, so that industry-wide sustainable development objectives are achieved. To this end, responsible business enterprises are taking leadership roles in industry associations, working with government and special interest groups to achieve positive results for both the enterprise and the stakeholders.

The monitoring of external developments is particularly complex for companies selling to export markets, and even more so for those with production facilities in several countries. Many multinational corporations subscribe to the International Chamber of Commerce principles on environmental management. These include adherence to international environmental performance standards. However, monitoring all the relevant international developments can be a daunting task. This external monitoring can be integrated into a firm's strategic management process, or else carried out as a separate exercise. Some corporations have social policy committees whose scope covers sustainable development issues. Others have environmental committees with a narrower focus.

References

Machan, T. R. (2007). *The Morality of Business: A Profession for Human Wealthcare*. Boston, Springer.

Murphy, P. E. (2002). *Marketing Ethics at the Millennium: Review, Reflections and Recommendations. Blackwell Guide to Business Ethics*. N. E. Bowie. Oxford, Blackwell: 165–185.

O'Neill, J. (1998). *The Market: Ethics, Knowledge and Politics*. London, Routledge.

Pinnington, A. H., R. Macklin, et al. (2007). *Introduction: ethical human resource management. Human Resource Management: Ethics and Employment*. A. H. Pinnington, R. Macklin and T. Campbell. Oxford, Oxford University Press: 1–22.

Bibliography

Albertson, Todd. (2007). *The Gods of Business: The Intersection of Faith and the Marketplace*. Los Angeles, CA: Trinity Alumni Press.

Allison, R. (2005). *The Birth of Spiritual Economics Spirituality and ethics in management*. L. Zsolnai. New York, Springer. 19: 61–74.

Anand, V. and C. C. Rosen (2008). "The Ethics of Organizational Secrets". *Journal of Management Inquiry* 17(2). 97–101.

Aristotle (1987). *Nicomachean Ethics*. New York, Prometheus Books

Armstrong, M. B. (2002). *Ethical Issues in Accounting. The Blcckwell guide to business ethics*. N. E. Bowie. Oxford, Blackwell: 145–157.

Badiou, A. (2001). *Ethics: An Fssay on the Understanding of Evil*. London, Verso.

Behrman, Jack N. (1988). *Essays on Ethics in Business and the Professions*. Englewood Cliffs, NJ: Prentice Hall.

Behrman, Jack N. (1988). *Essays on Ethics in Business and the Professions*. Englewood Cliffs, NJ: Prentice Hall.

Berle, A. A. and G. C. Means (2003). *The Modern Corporation and Private Property*. New Jersey, Transaction Publishers.

Bevan, D. (2008). *Continental Philosophy: A Grounded Theory Approach and the Emergence of Convenient and Inconvenient Ethics. Cutting Edge Issues in Business Ethics*. M. Painter-Morland and P. Werhane. Boston, Springer. 24: 131–152.

Boatright, J. R. (1999). *Finance ethics. A companion to business ethics. R. E. Frederic*. Oxford, Blackwell: 153–163.

Borgerson, J. L. and J. E. Schroeder (2008). *Building an Ethics of Visual Representation: Contesting Epistemic Closure in Marketing Communication. Cutting Edge Issues in Business Ethics*. M. P. Morland and P. Werhane. Boston, Springer: 87–108.

Bowie, Norman E. (1999). *Business Ethics, A Kantian Perspective*. Blackwell Publishing.

Bowie, Norman E. (1999). *Business Ethics, A Kantian Perspective*. Blackwell Publishing.

Boxall, P. and J. Purcell (2007). *Strategic management and human resources: the pursuit of productivity, exibility, and legitimacy. Human Resource Management: Ethics and Employment*. A. H. Pinnington, R. Macklin and T. Campbell. Oxford, Oxford University Press: 66–80.

Bradie, M. (1994). *The Secret Chain : Evolution and Ethics*. New York, State University of New York Press.

Brenkert, G. K. (1999). *Marketing ethics. A Companion to Business Ethics*. R. E. Frederic. Massachusetts, Blackwell: 178–193.

Cetina, K. K. and A. Preda, Eds. (2005). *The sociology of financial markets*. Oxford, Oxford University Press.

Collier, J. and R. Esteban (2007). "Corporate social responsibility and employee commitment". *Business Ethics: A European Review* 16(1). 19–33.

Cooter, R. and T. Ulen (1988). *Law and Economics*. New York, Harper Collins.

Cory, J. (2005). *Activist Business Ethics*. Boston, Springer.

Davidson, K. (2005). *Business Ethics. Ethics*. J. K. Roth. California, Salem Press Inc.: 181–187.

Dembinski, P. H., C. Lager, et al., Eds. (2006). *Enron and World Finance: A Case Study in Ethics*. New York, Palgrave.

Dobson, J. (1997). *Finance Ethics: The Rationality of Virtue*. New York, Rowman & Littlefield Publishers, Inc.

Drucker, P. (1981). "What is business ethics?" *The Public Interest Spring* (63). 18–36.

Duska, R. (1999). *Employee Rights. A companion to business ethics*. R. E. Frederic. Oxford, Blackwell: 257–268.

Dutfield, G. and U. Sunthersanen (2008). *Global Intellectual Property Law*. Cheltenham, Edward Elgar.

Friedman, K. S. (2003). *Myths of the Free market*. New York, Algora Publishing.

Galbraith, J. K. (1996). *The Good Society: The Humane Agenda*. Boston, Houghton-Mifflin Company.

George, Richard T. de (1999). *Business Ethics*. Prentice Hall.

Grabel, I. (2008). *Global finance and development: false starts, dead ends and social economic alternatives. The Elgar Companion to Social Economics*. J. B. Davis and W. Dolfsma. Cheltenham, Edward Elgar: 496–519.

Groucutt, J., P. Leadley, et al. (2004). *Marketing: essential principles, new realities*. London, Kogan Page.

Hartman, Laura (2004). *Perspectives in Business Ethics*. Burr Ridge, IL: McGraw-Hill.

Harwood, Sterling (1996). *Business as Ethical and Business as Usual*. Belmont, CA: The Thomson Corporation.

Jones, C., M. Parker, et al. (2005). *For Business Ethics: A Critical Text*. London, Routledge.

Koehn, D. (2002). *Ethical Issues in Human Resources. The blackwell guide to business ethics*. N. E. Bowie. Oxford, Blackwell: 225–243.

Lee, M. (2005). *Critiquing code of ethics. Critical Thinking in Human Resource Development*. C. Elliott and S. Turnbull. London, Routledge.

Machan, T. R. (2007). *The Morality of Business: A Profession for Human Wealthcare*. Boston, Springer.

Marcoux, A. (2009). *Business-Focused Business Ethics. Normative theory and Business Ethics*. J. Smith. New York, Rowman & Littlefield: 17–34.

Maxwell, J. C. (2003). *There is no such thing as business ethics*. New York, Warner Books.

Michelman, F. I. (1982). *Ethics, Economics, and the Law of Property. Nomos: Ethics, Economics, and the Law*. J. R. Pennock and J. W. Chapman. New York, New York University Press. 24: 3–40.

Moore, G. (2009). *Virtue Ethics and Business Organizations. Normative theory and business ethics*. J. Smith. New York, Rowman & Littlefield: 35–60.

Murphy, P. E. (2002). *Marketing Ethics at the Millennium: Review, Reflections and Recommendations. Blackwell Guide to Business Ethics*. N. E. Bowie. Oxford, Blackwell: 165–185.

O'Neill, J. (1998). *The Market: Ethics, Knowledge and Politics*. London, Routledge.

Pinnington, A. H., R. Macklin, et al. (2007). *Introduction: ethical human resource management. Human Resource Management: Ethics and Employment*. A. H. Pinnington, R. Macklin and T. Campbell. Oxford, Oxford University Press: 1–22.

Program, G. G. (2004). *Business Ethics: A manual for managing a responsible business enterprise in emerging market economies*. Washington DC, Good Governance Program, US Department of Commerce.

Samuels, W., J (1977). *Ideology in Economics Modern Economic Thought*. S. Weintraub. Oxford, Blackwell: 467–484.

Smith, J., Ed. (2009). *Normative Theory and Business Ethics*. New York, Rowman & Littlefield

Solomon, R. (1999). *Business ethics and virtue. A Companion to Business Ethics*. R. Frederick. Oxford, Blackwell: 30–37.

Snoeyenbos, M. and J. Humber (1999). *Utilitarianism and business ethics. A Companion to Business Ethics*. R. E. Frederic. Massachusetts, Blackwell: 17–29.

Steelman, A. (2008). *Intellectual Property. The Encyclopedia of Libertarianism*. R. Hamowy, J. Kuznicki and A. Steelman. Los Angeles, Sage Reference: 249–250.

Transparency International (2009). "Global Corruption Report 2009: Corruption and Private Sector. (A Report by Transparency International)." Cambridge, Cambridge University Press.

Ulrich, P. (2008). *Integrative Economic Ethics: Foundations of a Civilized Market Economy*. Cambridge, Cambridge University Press.

Välimäki, M. (2005). *The Rise of Open Source Licensing: A Challenge to the Use of Intellectual Property in the Software Industry*. Helsinki, Turre Publishing.

Walsh, A. J. (2007). *HRM and the ethics of commodied work in a market economy. Human Resource Management: Ethics and Employment*. A. H. Pinnington, R. Macklin and T. Campbell. Oxford, Oxford University Press: 102–118.

Index